A fascinating sojourn you will never forget.

Join Dr. Peters in his inspired mission that began just after World War II and continues today. Follow him as his World Neighbors ministry, on a shoestring budget, put their Christian faith into practice as they reach out to the poor and destitute in 41 Third World countries. You will be uplifted as these people regain their dignity and learn to help themselves. You will share the intrigue with Dr. Peters as he experiences numerous confrontations with danger and interacts with significant people, both great and small:

- Travel to India to meet Jawaharlal Nehru and other top leaders; rejoice with once famine-stricken villagers as they prosper and are touched by the message of Christ
- Visit Africa — From Ethiopia, for a meeting with Haile Selassie, to Tanzania for a chat with a witch doctor!
- Fight on the home front with Dr. Peters as he attempts to raise funds amid Washington's bureaucracy

Here's a behind-the-scenes look at history in the making and a world most of us will never know even remotely. It comes alive in *Loving God Isn't Enough*.

Loving God Isn't Enough

John L. Peters

Power Books

Fleming H. Revell Company
Old Tappan, New Jersey

Scripture quotations in this volume are from the King James Version of the Bible.

Peters, John Leland.
Loving God isn't enough.

Bibliography: p.
1. World Neighbors (Organization) 2. Economic assistance—Developing countries. 3. Economic development projects—Developing countries. I. Title.
HC60.P397   1989   361.7′63′091724   89-10302
ISBN   0-8007-5321-6

Copyright © 1989 by John L. Peters
Published by the Fleming H. Revell Company
Old Tappan, New Jersey 07675
Printed in the United States of America

Contents

Then . . . a lawyer, asked him a question, tempting him, and saying, Master, which is the great commandment in the law? Jesus said unto him, Thou shalt love the Lord thy God with all thy heart, and with all thy soul, and with all thy mind. This is the first and great commandment. And the second is like unto it, Thou shalt love thy neighbour as thyself. On these two commandments hang all the law and the prophets.

Matthew 22:35–40

Prologue

In the face of record-breaking Western productivity, millions who live in the Third World remain gripped in a deepening spiral of poverty and hunger.

This tragic fact provides a bitter commentary on four decades of "aid and development" undertaken with the highest of hopes, by unilateral and multilateral agencies of government. Though they have spent well over $100 billion in an effort to reach and change the lot of the underprivileged masses, the most impressive result has been the widening gulf between the already prosperous and the perpetually poor.

Therefore we should not feel surprise that of the 159 countries that comprise the United Nations, the operating democracies are an overwhelmed minority. In many of the rest, authoritarian or totalitarian governments have established and are taking steps to continue their regimes. There are, it is true, some promising signs of change. But such change remains tentative and contingent on many factors.

The following is the founder's account of a grass-roots movement that over the last thirty-seven years and with an incredibly small amount of private funds has planted or nourished the self-help initiative in forty-one countries of the Third World. The results—in terms of increased food production, improved health, voluntary family planning, and greater personal income—have brought the seeds of self-reliance to not less than 25 million people. That movement believes that its task—the implementation of the Judeo-Christian imperative to love one's neighbor as oneself—is just beginning.

I have drawn the data herein from four decades of diaries, logs, records, and reports. In addition, especially during my travels away from home, each night I recorded—for the edification or amusement of my wife and son—all the noteworthy details of the day's events. This included, in particular, all meetings and conversations with individuals of note or interest.

I have also taken the liberty of including occasional excerpts from my book *Cry Dignity!*[1]

It is my prayerful hope that the following record will encourage any who may have looked at our troubled world and said, "But what can I do that will make any real difference?"

Loving God Isn't Enough

1

Incubation of a Good Idea

My journey actually began in the Philippine Visayans as World War II dragged to its bloody close. I was chaplain with the Fortieth Infantry Division—one segment of which had been ordered to neutralize the threat posed by several thousand Japanese Royal Marines, who had "dug in" on the big island of Mindanao. So I attached myself to my line companies as they made their way toward the rain forest where our forces had encountered the fiercest resistance.

On the day we began climbing the muddy slopes that led to our destination, a hot meal was flown up to us along with the mail. As I lay in the tall grass, reading those heart-melting letters from home, I happened to glance at a lad who had more mail than any of us.

He was an Infantry Replacement who had just joined the outfit. While he had traveled by slow convoy, his mail, coming by plane, had accumulated. Like a starving man at a feast, he reveled in the wonderful words from his loved ones.

Then he came to a letter in a manila envelope. He tore it open and read it. His jaw dropped. He looked up, saw me watching, and brought the letter over.

"Look at this, Chaplain. It's one for the books."

Together we read the letter from his draft board in Tennessee. It told him that, since he was the only able-bodied man on his father's farm, they had decided to classify him 4-F. He didn't have to go. We laughed.

"This is something you can tell your grandchildren one of these days," I said.

A few hours later, on a slippery trail deep in the forest, an artillery round burst squarely on top of us. I held the lad from Tennessee in my arms while, ripped with shrapnel, he bled to death.

That night in my muddy foxhole, my fatigues stiff with the blood of the boy who wasn't supposed to be there, I said to God, "If I get out of this thing alive, I'm going to do something, if I can, to keep this from happening again and again." I was sick of violence, of young boys killing and being killed, of "accidents" that forever took away their hopes and dreams.

Not only our American soldiers suffered and died. Throughout Asia I had seen the pinched, hopeless face of poverty and want, hunger and despair. From this fuel violence was so often ignited.

The war finally ended, and the Fortieth Infantry Division was sent to Korea, to expedite the departure of the Japanese and to help the South Koreans establish a representative government. But even when—in the little towns and cities—we could secure the election of a clearly popular choice, Communist execution squads almost always ended the new leader's brief tenure in a burst of gunfire. Refugees fleeing North Korea also brought reports of almost unbelievable ferocity as the advancing Red army of Kim Il Sung sought to exterminate all religious and intellectual leadership.

After a while I came home; the scene blessedly changed. Though the Orient seemed far away, my foxhole promise still persistently nagged at my conscience. *What can I do that really would make a difference?* I wondered helplessly.

I finished my doctorate at Yale; taught for a time at Methodist-related Oklahoma City University; "filled the pulpit" on an interim basis at Saint Luke's United Methodist Church. One Sunday, after listening to General MacArthur address the joint houses of Congress on the seismic events underway in Asia, I preached a sermon titled "Let's Deal With Basic Issues." I talked about the things I'd seen, but I spoke mostly about the things I felt: that the gulf between the rich and the wretched was intolerable; that we were brothers *to*, not keepers *of*, the world's needy; that we must learn to do things *with*, not *to*—or even *for*—others; that *they* must share in electing priorities and procedures; and that—constrained and guided by the Spirit of Christ—we must begin *now*. The message's parameters came from outside the borders of my knowledge or experience.

Amazingly, my broadcasted sermon elicited an immediate and statewide response. Phones at the church never stopped ringing. An organization began to take shape; funds were pledged. It was voted to "back John Peters 100 percent in what he wants to do." When they saw I didn't know what to do, they sent me to New York and Washington.

"When you've found the answer," they said, "come back and tell us."

It seemed logical to me that our ambassador to the United Nations should have some basic answers. So once ensconced in a little hotel on New York's Twenty-eighth Street, I called and asked for an early appointment.

"He might," said his secretary, "be able to see you for a few minutes this morning. But you had better hurry. He must leave soon for some meetings with the Security Council."

So I found a taxi, promised the driver some extra bucks if we made it, and into the treaclelike traffic we plunged. But a heavy foot and a loud horn were no match for the strangled streets of Manhattan. We pulled up before the red brick structure at Number One Park Avenue minutes after the ambassador had gone.

However the ambassador had told someone else to see me.

"Just who do you represent?" this senior official asked, pointing me to a brown leather chair.

He really should have said whom, I thought in passing. But as he continued to cram papers into an already bulging briefcase I told him how it all started.

"So that's who we are—business people, church people, housewives, professionals; you name it. We're private, voluntary, interfaith, and interracial. We have no ax to grind. The one thing that unites us is our desire to find a way to help people in the underdeveloped areas to help themselves, without depriving them of their dignity."

For a moment or two he stopped packing. He pushed his fingers through his short, graying hair and cleared his throat.

"You're right, you know. The really hungry world—the billion or more just a meal or so away from starvation—live in what we're beginning to call the Less Developed Countries. They need more than relief. They need to get on their own feet. I'm glad *somebody's* thinking along the lines you mentioned. I just wonder if you know the size and complexity of the job you're taking on.

"There is," he continued as he crossed the room and jerked open a drawer, "another side of this you may not have considered. Have you, for instance, ever read 'The Paley Report'?"

" 'The Paley Report'?" I gulped. "What's that?"

He grinned.

"Oh, don't feel too bad. The report came out in 1945. Now, here it is 1951, and I don't suppose one in a thousand Americans has ever heard of it. And that's a shame. For that report, named after William S. Paley, who chaired the committee that produced it, ought to be *must* reading for every citizen. In fact, it's going to be the substance of my talk to a women's association in Connecticut this very evening. As you see, I'm getting ready now to leave."

So for the next quarter hour, as he continued organizing last-minute notes and dashing off last-minute memos, he told me just how vulnerable, how dependent, our great nation really is.

"Did you know that a light tank requires over 6,000 pounds of bauxite? Well, we import sixty-five percent of our bauxite. For armor plate and aircraft we need tungsten and cobalt—and we import fifty-two percent of our tungsten and almost ninety percent of our cobalt. We can't make a pound of steel without manganese—and we import ninety-three percent of our manganese. We import ninety-nine percent of our nickel, one hundred percent of our graphite, one hundred percent of our chromium, and one hundred percent of our tin.

"And, look, more than seventy-three percent of all these materials come from the underdeveloped areas. Without them, we couldn't make automobiles or telephones or machine tools—to say nothing of mounting a defense program."

He handed me a report listing all this and slammed his briefcase on the desk. Then he glared at me as though I had just voted for isolationism.

"The truth is we can't live without imports—especially imports from Asia, Africa, and Latin America. If *we* don't know this," he concluded, shaking his finger under my nose, "the Communists do. We'd better find out fast."

Finally it was obvious that the interview must come to an end. I struggled up from my chair.

"I'm really sorry I've got to run," said the official as we parted. "All I can do is wish you and your associates well. For in the areas you want to help, the United States needs all the friends we can make or keep."

With that he was gone.

I called a good-bye after him, stopped for a moment to thank the receptionist, then hunted for the subway line that would drop me nearest to my hotel.

How did it happen, I thought as we rocketed through the bowels of the city, *that neither I nor most of my friends have ever heard about this?*

But I had scant time for reflection. The next few days were filled with appointments: some of the newborn agencies of the United Nations, the Committee on World Literacy, the Christian Medical Council, and Agricultural Missions.

In Washington I found my way to a "temporary" World War II building where Dr. Henry Bennett was trying to put together Point Four (later AID). "I want to keep this program small," he said. "Grass roots. But it's not going to be easy."

Over at the Capitol, Dr. Walter Judd—former medical missionary to China, then congressman from Minnesota and ranking member of the Committee on Foreign Affairs—came off the floor of the House to meet me, listen, and say, "Why what you have in mind is what I've been asking for for twenty years."

I came home and reported to my friends what I had learned on my trip. We began to raise money. Within six months we had raised several thousand dollars—too little to do much, too much to do nothing.

"Look," said the devoted group of men and women I had gathered around me, "we can't sit on this money. We need to start a project. If we do, we'll need someone to give it on-the-ground attention— someone who can check it out, follow it up, help it get over the humps, and be sure that funds are used wisely. Most of us are business and professional people. We can't walk away from our responsibilities.

"Now you got us into this. And the university could surely find a replacement for you. So here's what we've agreed on. If you'll take a leave of absence, go overseas whenever necessary, and give continuing oversight to the whole program, we'll see that your family doesn't starve."

They had made me an offer I couldn't refuse.

18

2

The Testing Ground

So in January, 1952, I found myself on a Pan American Clipper felicitously named *The Golden Rule*, bound for India. From many sources we had heard about an agricultural missionary named Jack DeValois, who had been well received by his Indian associates and had written books on poultry and goats. He had even started an agricultural institute.

But he operated on a shoestring—a few hundred dollars a year in addition to his very limited salary. He couldn't send the men and women he had trained out into the desperately needy countryside.

We had written him, and he had written back. But neither of us could fully understand the nature, goals, and procedures of the other. Finally, I went to meet him and his associates.

Another passenger on my flight was Chester Bowles, United States ambassador to India and Nepal. From time to time—as the stewardess permitted me to slip from my coach seat into first class—we visited. He was, for all his rank and responsibilities, gracious in his manner, generous with his time, and avidly interested.

"What you are telling me, Mr. Peters, is one of the most hopeful things I've heard in a long time. When you get to New Delhi, you must come out to the embassy. I want you to meet some of my people.

"Let me encourage you," he went on, "to get out to the villages. I think you'll see that, in the right hands, a great deal can be done with very little. It would be hard to raise production by ten percent in Japan. But it should be no problem to raise food production in India by thirty percent. You can't believe how antiquated some of the methods are!

"You're coming at a very critical time, you know. The elections are nearing their close, and the Communists are making a strong showing. To keep India out of their hands, the new five-year plan has simply *got* to work. Nehru realizes this. And he's a good man, greatly admired. But it's going to take hard-headed planning, effort, and discipline.

"Nehru," the ambassador continued, "is making a great race. It looks as if he will have about forty percent of the vote, and the Communists will get about twenty-eight percent. That means India will have a factional government—like France, but without the political sophistication of the French.

"Of course, if India should actually go Communist, you could expect the Middle East and Southeast Asia to follow. Certainly America's strategic position would be seriously impaired."

He shifted in his seat, pausing, I thought, to wonder why he was telling me all this. Suddenly he sat up straight.

"It's high time Americans woke up!" he burst out. "I'd like to see a hundred good county agents out in the rural areas right now—with two hundred more coming just as soon as we could get them here.

"Of course," he said slowly, "they would have to put aside any feeling of superiority. They'd have to have the right kind of motivation. That's why I'm so pleased to learn about you and your friends. I'm convinced there's an increasing need for nongovernmental aid— the kind, in fact, you've been describing. For this job we face is simply immense. And it's critical. But please don't misunderstand me, I believe it's possible."

The long hours of the plane trip passed. Finally, I struggled through the bustling customs of Palam Airport. New sensations engulfed me: people, voices, colors, noise, odors. The contrasts were overwhelming.

As I rode into town in an up-to-the-minute airport limousine, families of big, gray monkeys bounced from the roadside trees and scampered beside our wheels. While the tires of transcontinental planes screamed their protests before leaving the tarmac, languid camels, tall against the sky, pulled tiny plows through tired soil. A row of vultures—their bare necks folded into the feathers of their scruffy breasts—stared impassively at us from the spotted ledge of an ancient limestone temple, while smart apartments, built only yesterday, stood at proud attention as we forded the river of bicycles flowing down New Delhi's wide thoroughfares.

It was late; I was tired; and the hotel clerk was unable to locate my reservations. Finally a room was found for me at the Maidens Hotel in Old Delhi. *Is it*, I wondered, *the Indian version of the YWCA?*

Once there, I flung myself onto a mattress as unyielding as astroturf, checked to see if I'd broken any ribs, found no fractures, and fell asleep.

Horace Holmes, head of the Point Four program in India, rescued me. For two days this transplanted Tennesseean and his wife, Evelyn, entertained me in their own home.

Life magazine had just done a full-page spread on Horace, depicting him as a kind of hero in India's assault on rural poverty. The article was a good one—obviously intended as a tribute. But a photograph showed him stretched at full length on a divan, presumably giving directions to his subservient Indian counterparts. For Horace, it was a major embarrassment.

Like the editors of *Life*, I needed to know a great deal more about India's ethos and sensibilities. But to whom should I turn for help?

Horace, who had seen rural India close up, was a valued monitor.

Later, at the embassy, social and economic attaché Evelyn Hersey virtually echoed Ambassador Bowles's words. "If Point Four does all it can do, and Nehru does all he can do, and people like you do all you can do, we've got a fifty-fifty chance."

An invitation to visit Methodist Bishop and Mrs. J. Wascom Pickett came as a Godsend. In the cool interior of their tree-shrouded home over tea and biscuits, I garnered another glimpse of India, rich in anecdotal detail.

There I heard of mass movements among various tribal groups, sagas of the sons and daughters of rajahs who, finding Christ, had also found great persecution. I was told of the loving mediation afforded by Christians to Hindu and Moslem alike during the bloody massacres sparked by the recent partition that only five years earlier had formed India and Pakistan. I learned of conversations with Jawaharlal Nehru who, repelled by the violence of Krishna Menon's attack on all things Christian, had told his fiery associate, "You make me ashamed to be called a Hindu."

There was also the story of Dr. Ambedkar. Bhimrao Ramji Ambedkar had been born an untouchable. But his brilliance (and the sponsorship of the ruler of Baroda) had won him scholarships in the United States, Britain, and Germany. After a successful legal career, he became, in 1947, the law minister of the new government of India.

But all his life—because he was a harijan, a member of the untouchable caste—he had been humiliated and excluded by his high-caste associates. So as he assumed a major role in framing India's constitution, he helped outlaw discrimination against untouchables.

It takes more than well-intentioned constitutional provisions, however, to alter long-established social customs. Finally, in 1951, Dr. Ambedkar announced from his home in Bombay that he was giving up his Hinduism. The news was still fresh when I visited Bishop Pickett in January, 1952.

"When I saw the announcement in the paper," said the bishop, "I immediately made reservations to fly to Bombay. I had known Ambedkar for years, and I was sure he would see me."

He was right. And Dr. Ambedkar listened carefully as the bishop urged him to become a Christian. Finally, he responded. "Bishop, when I look at Jesus Christ, I say, 'That's the one I would like to follow.' But when I look at the warring Christian sects of the state of Bombay, I say, 'Good Lord, deliver me.' " In time, Dr. Ambedkar became a Buddhist, taking several hundred thousand of his harijan followers with him.

The evening was full of these colorful accounts. But I was eager to get on to my original assignment. So I wired Jack DeValois, at Katpadi, told him I was on my way, and caught a plane to Madras.

Madras State (now Tamil Nadu) was at that time in the grip of a famine. For four hot, long years the monsoons had failed. The land was parched; people and animals were dying; millions were hungry. Encouraged by agitators, bands of desperate men roamed the countryside—pillaging, robbing, and killing. Travel, especially at night, became so precarious that even the huge lorries moved in clustering convoys.

No wonder Jack DeValois—tall, cordial, and authoritative—sped us swiftly through airport formalities and onto the highway that snaked its way west toward the Malabar coast. We had ninety miles to cover before we reached Katpadi, and the velvet darkness of an Indian night would wrap us round long before we got there.

The leaves of the tamarind trees rustled nervously in the dry night wind as we pulled off the highway and scurried down the long drive toward the mission center, a spacious, two-story "bungalow"— home, office, and hostel—that had been built with an appreciation for the heat and an eye for durability. Now, carved from the dusk by the probing starlight, its pale bulk loomed eerily in the distance. As we drew nearer, from deep within its wide rooms, oil lamps flickered an invitation.

At the door Jack's wife, Dr. Bernadine—not only the attractive mistress of the home but also the highly regarded head of the ENT section of the famed Christian Medical Hospital College and at Vellore, some ten miles away—greeted us. I hoped that, travel-weary and begrimed as I was, I passed her inspection. She made me feel I did.

As we went inside, she told her husband there had been a bit of a diversion. That afternoon a cheetah had dashed into the compound, pounced on one of the dogs and, with it, escaped back into the hills. Oh, yes, a large cobra had also crawled under the house. Presumably, it was still there.

On that happy note, we went to bed.

The following afternoon came the formal meeting with Jack's board of directors—all of them missionaries and pastors. Within a couple of hours, the initial stiffness vanished, and we discovered that we really liked each other. Before long a project—improved agriculture, maternal and child health, literacy—was in prospect.

Once we had clearly defined the objectives, established a timetable, and determined a budget, I agreed we would send them funds to be disbursed quarterly, with successive payments contingent on acceptable reports of progress. They, in turn, would provide local personnel and day-by-day administration. Additional transport, equipment, or stock would be made available on a revolving loan basis. I would make periodic calls for inspection and counsel. Everything seemed in order.

It occurred to me, however, that the people I *really* should see were the intended recipients of the project's benefits. Back in Oklahoma we had said our work should be "from the bottom up." Now, if we were to impose some preconceived structure on a people who had had no voice in its character, wasn't that "from the top down?" Wasn't that being our brother's keeper without ever having become our brother's brother?

So I asked for a meeting with the villagers themselves. Did *they* want what we had been talking about? If so, what were they prepared to do about it? If not, what *did* they want? To find out, an evening meeting, with representatives of several villages in attendance, was arranged.

So in an old Land Rover that had bounced me over rut-riven roads, I at last came face-to-face with those toward whom—so many years and miles ago—I had been impelled.

Before dismounting, I looked at them—thin, ragged, hungry, and proud. I now knew something of their immense need, their bank-ruptcy of resources. On the trip south from New Delhi, I had read a report from a bureau of the Indian government, which stated that half of India's people would spend no more than twenty cents a month on consumer goods. As I read those figures, I had leaned back in my seat and thought of the creature comforts I took so much for granted—commonplace back home, fabulous out here.

Now as I saw the people described in the report, statistics suddenly metamorphosed into flesh and blood. *Twenty cents a month!* Who was I to talk to these impoverished brothers about "self-help"? What bootstraps did *they* have to pull themselves up by? Surely *charity*—unqualified and unrestrained—was love's response. In spite of all we had said about self-help, surely this seemed a time for giveaways.

But continuing "relief"—handed out by the well-intentioned rich to the ever-supplicating poor—was not the arrangement God had planned for this human family of His. There had to be a way for even these impoverished souls to stand one day on their own two feet—blessed, self-reliant, and independent. The rains *would* return. There *would* be a better tomorrow. The part of wisdom, as well as faith, was to anticipate and plan for it.

As I stepped from the Land Rover a sea of dark faces—impassive, weatherworn, turban crowned—lifted toward me. Brown eyes pierced the evening haze, exploring, probing. I suddenly felt conscious of my whiteness, so stark that I felt unfinished, anemic, and raw.

The introductions, in Tamil, were mercifully short. Then I was speaking, trying to explain, through my trusted interpreter, what our little band, back in the American Southwest, really wanted to do.

What we had in mind, I said, was some sort of *partnership*—a "joint venture" we called it back in the United States (my interpreter was having real problems with this concept). We wanted to do something *with* them, not *to* them or *for* them. We had been told that they needed more food, better clothing, better houses, and better health care. We believed such things were right and possible. But to bring them about called for a great deal of cooperation.

"First," I said, "we are going to need God's cooperation. We are praying and expecting that the monsoons will return, and we will once again plant crops and reap harvests. Second, we are going to need the cooperation of the authorities. We believe that will be forthcoming. For India is committed to a great nation-building program, and Mahatma Gandhi has insisted that it begin in the villages. Third, we are going to need the cooperation of the people on the land. They must want improvement enough to give their time and thought and labor to those things that would make improvement possible. These people are, of course, you. It is *your* program and will succeed or fail because of what you do—or don't do.

"If this kind of cooperation can be secured, I can promise another—the helping hand of the people I represent. They are people like yourselves. They make their livings the same way you make yours—by working for it. They *could* spend all their money on themselves and their children. But they truly want to see you succeed, and they are ready to join hands with you when the help they can offer will make it possible for you to complete the job you have already begun."

I could tell by their faces they didn't understand what I was trying to say. And I was having more than a little trouble saying it. An outright gift, some sort of day-to-day employment, a proposal to build a road or dig a well—these things they could have comprehended. But *partnership?* What did *that* mean? How would it work? Why was it offered?

In fact, the first question from one of the village headmen aimed directly at that point. He stepped forward, and from deep within the wind-grooved leather of his falconlike face, his eyes sought mine. "Why," he said, "would people who have never seen us, who have never heard our names, want to help us as you say?"

Suddenly I was back in the United Nations ambassador's office, hearing an official's sharp voice saying, "You say you want to help the developing areas. Why?" Just as I had paused then, I paused now. How should I answer this Tamil-speaking son of the soil? Would I be believed if I said anything other than "intelligent self-interest"?

For that was what I had been previously told to say by some friends in the State Department. "You may feel otherwise, John, but it is the *only* thing that will be accepted."

This is what Chester Bowles *had* said in a Bombay press conference at the Taj Mahal Hotel a few days before—only to be pilloried by the left-wing newspaper *Blitz* with the headline: "Bowles Bowled Out; Admits U.S. Aid Purely Self-Interest."

It wasn't that I feared a similar reaction. I knew that *my* people, at least, had *not* responded to my sermon out of self-interest. They had, instead, become convinced that helping the world's distressed was a compelling part of the religion they professed. If that also helped build a more stable, livable world, well and good. But their motivation was not the fruit of an irrational fear. It was the flower of a meaningful faith.

How could I make that clear to this throng of strangers? Were these men Hindu? Moslem? Christian? I didn't know. All I knew was that I didn't want to alienate them. For I was sure God intended us to be building new bridges, not strengthening old walls. Perhaps later, over those new bridges, could flow a traffic that would minister to heretofore-unmet spiritual needs. But what about *their* needs and *my* needs—right now?

An inspiration struck me—or so I thought. I smiled into the face of my waiting questioner. I knew that I had the suitable answer. "The people who have sent me here have come to see that being in one world together is like being in a ship together. When part of that ship is in trouble, *all* the ship is in trouble. So," I tried to continue, "your troubles are our troubles; your needs are our needs."

But my interpreter tugged at my elbow. "Sir," he said, "these people have never seen a ship. They don't know what you're talking about."

I was dumbfounded. Surely *everybody* knew what a ship was! But as I looked about me, I knew my interpreter was right. Of what use was a ship to people who never dreamed of traveling more than ten miles from the village in which they were born—and who were a hundred miles from an ocean they could not even imagine?

If I couldn't talk about a ship, what *could* I talk about? I knew they understood what an ox cart was. But an ox cart just wouldn't carry the analogy. Completely out of similes, I was driven to the explanation I should have offered in the first place. For I had long ago, in a life-changing personal experience, committed myself to God and to His will. So I took a deep breath and started again.

"My friends, the people who sent me here to talk with you have done so because their faith teaches them that, in order to love and serve their God, they must love and help their neighbors. They now realize that—even though they haven't heard your names or seen your faces—you *are* their neighbors. And they have sent me here to learn how to make that love real."

I stopped.

Without prior thought or prompt recognition, I had just enunciated what would—from that time forward—be the high commission of my life: to find out how love can be expressed in ways that build up rather than tear down, that challenge rather than condone, that fortify rather than enfeeble. That tough ideal would be my holy grail. I had glimpsed its outline as I preached the sermon at Saint Luke's. I would see its structure as many hands wrought its completion.

But just now I wondered whether I had stumbled into alienation. *Now they know that our motivation is spiritual,* I thought. *And they are probably saying, "So he's a sub-rosa missionary after all." I've probably lost them before we even had a chance to start.*

I was completely wrong. A great wave of acceptance rolled like a white-capped breaker toward me. The artful reference to ships could never penetrate the precincts of their minds, but the simple offer of love had plumbed the depths of their souls. The walls were down, the way was open.

So began a project that would be our laboratory—our trial-and-error learning experience. I felt encouraged. We now had a competent operational base, a dedicated corps of workers, a receptive company of participants. It was a good beginning.

But we had yet to discover most of the answers. In fact, we didn't even know most of the *questions.* Did we really know how to motivate? How and whom to enlist? How to be beneficially productive? How to "institutionalize" what might prove worth keeping? How to withdraw when we were no longer needed? And, of course, how to raise the money our work would require?

All this, and so much more, we would simply have to find out, mainly from the people with whom we worked. I could only hope that the project would survive while we learned. I was only sure that God hadn't started something He didn't intend to finish.

Yet before I left South India, my faith was sorely tried. What hope could I offer the old man and his son, whom I met on a brief journey into the countryside? Burned black by the sun under whose pitiless rays they labored, they were as thin and gnarled as the mango trees they were now cutting down. For the drought had killed the orchard, their last source of food and income.

We stopped to visit. They spoke of how badly they needed rain. "What will you do now?" I asked as the dust whirled at our feet.

The old man straightened his ragged, soiled turban. "I will," he said in a flat, lifeless voice, "try to sell the wood."

"And after that?"

He turned for a moment to glance at his son, who, drooped and sallow, stood looking at the ground. Then he turned back to me, and silently, fatalistically, he shrugged.

We went on.

At another stop we found one of the few wells that still contained a little water. From it the owner was irrigating the tiny bit of land the limited water would still reach. In the heavy harness, usually worn by bullocks, four women strained to pull the great leathern bucket to and from the deep, deep well. I couldn't keep from asking, "Why do you use women instead of bullocks?"

He barely looked up. "Because women don't eat as much."

Against this bleak background our first project began. The outlook was desperate, but not hopeless. We secured some "relief supplies" and started "food for work" projects—building roads, deepening wells, beginning wide-scale reforestation. The land was made ready for the next monsoons, which did indeed come. Youth clubs wrought local miracles in poultry programs and village sanitation. Visiting nurses brought better health and improved nutrition to mothers and children.

It was a hand up, not a handout. That hand, extended in love, bred a meaningful response. We were, it actually seemed, building from the bottom up.

Yet in the midst of all the advances, a growing conviction that we were still working through essentially authoritarian channels remained. It was from the missionary—or his appointed adjutants—that the major decisions flowed: when and where to work, what and how to do.

One hot day I watched one of the "straw bosses" in action. He was capable, intelligent, and dedicated—and of a higher caste than his associates. Determined to meet schedules in record time, he barked his orders like a true drill sergeant.

I stood it just so long. After a while I remonstrated, "You're handling these people like some army work detail. When are you going to start building a *team*—letting them make some of the decisions, letting them take some of the responsibilities?"

He looked at me in amazement. "Do you want this project completed or not? If I wait for each one of them to put in his say-so, we'll *never* get this job done."

I knew we needed to find a different channel of operation.

Meanwhile another factor troubled me. For I couldn't forget the counsel of a very wise man.

His name was John Nuveen. His vocation was the sale of municipal bonds.

But his avocation was international affairs. After World War II, he had been made chief of the Economic Cooperation Administration (which directed the Marshall Plan) in Greece. Assigned the rank of minister to Belgium and Luxembourg, he had helped guide the economic recovery of Europe. And, in the process, he had noted the impact—for good or ill—of shifting regimes.

On one occasion we had urged him to become an active director of World Neighbors. He asked for time to think it over. Later, as I passed through Chicago, I called to give him my greeting. He invited me to lunch.

As we finished an excellent meal, he leaned back in his chair. "John," he said, "I like you and your friends. But you don't seem to be sufficiently concerned about influencing the character of governments—here or abroad. It's been my observation that the wrong people at the top can wipe out in a few minutes all that the right people at the bottom have been able to do in years of creative work."

I didn't have an answer. As World Neighbors didn't have a

"political" agenda, John Nuveen decided not to become a director.

However, I perceived the real wisdom in what he had said. Now I was in India, at the sociological "bottom," engaged in "creative work." *But what about the "people at the top"?* I wondered. *Would they be likely to sustain or destroy what we might accomplish?* I decided to learn what I could.

Someone had once told me about the Bharat Sevak Samaj. It was, they said, the social service arm of the Congress Party, a quasigovernmental program whose goals were to inspire and mobilize private groups and individuals for the great Community Development Program India was undertaking.

So when opportunity afforded, I made my way to their nest of offices at the Theatre Communications Building in midtown New Delhi. The first man I met was Major T. Ramachandra.

He appeared to be in his sixties—small, intense, direct, and completely devoted to his task and vision. In his homespun khadi, he didn't look like a major, which he had been; he looked like a Gandhian, which he was. Turning from what he was doing— recycling old envelopes for interoffice memos, he introduced himself. I liked him immediately and immensely.

We talked for a few minutes about India, World Neighbors, and the Bharat Sevak Samaj. Then he introduced me to his associates. What with introductions and conversation, the time sped by. Then Major Ramachandra looked at his watch and blanched. "I'm due at a meeting at the prime minister's," he said to me. "Would you like to come with me?" I would.

So in a tiny cab—a revamped motorcycle—we sped out to the official residence. We were hurried through the formal entry and were ushered down a brief flight of stairs to the wide enclosure in the rear.

There, in a garden girt by high walls and flowering shrubs, sat Jawaharlal Nehru. Handsome as a matinee idol, dressed in jodhpurlike trousers and a casual jacket, with aquiline features and the golden-tan skin of a true Kashmiri Brahman, he was perched on the edge of a chair. Men and women—representatives of the work-camp leadership of the Bharat Sevak Samaj—formed an adoring circle around him. The women wore saris, modest and proletarian. The men wore khadar. Some had on Gandhi caps. I was the only "outsider," conspicuous in my dark, Western suit. We all sat on small carpets, spread over the green, manicured grass.

The prime minister's speech was in Hindi, of course. Major Ramachandra was good enough to give me its gist.

Essentially, Nehru said, "There is an immense task that lies ahead. Poverty must be overcome. The needs of the village poor are paramount concerns. Agriculture is basic. India simply must free herself from her reliance on others. In personal relations, we must recognize how badly we treat each other. Caste is, of course, part of our problem. But so is our so-called spirituality—which is not that at all. Much of what passes for piety is pure selfishness. We get so wrapped up in our personal needs and inner problems that we simply go blind to the needs of others. Let us never get so accustomed to poverty and degradation that it doesn't move us."

He waited for a few questions and then continued. "The Congress Party is proud of the BSS. But perhaps we have become too satisfied with simply proclaiming our good intentions. We must plan, yes. But we must also *do*. It's now time to stop talking and go to work!"

I was amazed at the prime minister's stagecraft. He was absolute master of the scene. His rapt audience hung on his every word. He knew just when to inject a humorous reference—and break the tension of his rebukes and injunctions. He permitted interruptions and listened patiently as they came.

But there was ample evidence that he was deeply tired. When he spoke, he was animated and youthful. When he relaxed, as others talked, he looked spent, worn, and world-weary—as well he might be. For India's entire well-being was in the hands of an elderly few.

Most decisions of any consequence also had to receive the prime minister's personal review.

Nehru himself was no mere politician, no glib power broker. I recalled what Bishop Pickett, who had known him for years, had told me. "Actually," the bishop had said, "although Nehru is secularist by his own definition, he is a man of far greater depth than he admits. In some ways he's greater than Gandhi. He says only what he means, and he means what he says."

By now the conference had come to an end. The prime minister, with an indulgent smile, had risen from his chair. All of us instantly rose. As Mr. Nehru came in our direction, Major Ramachandra insisted on introducing me. We exchanged *namastes*—"greetings," in Hindi—and I was asked to relate something about our movement-to-be. I tried to make it brief.

"Now let me understand this," said the prime minister, pulling his eyebrows together, "you hope to build world peace through world neighbors?"

"I suppose you could put it that way."

"Well, I must say that for me, peace would be a far greater likelihood if it weren't for my neighbors!"

We all laughed. My laugh was rueful. For Nehru made me realize that proximity is not necessarily fraternity. "Getting to know you" may, in fact, mean coming to resent you. It all depended.

Reassured as I was that the "man at the top" would not deliberately destroy what we were attempting at the bottom, I still had some lingering concerns. How much, for instance, was Nehru influenced by his virulently anti-American defense minister? I asked this question of a prominent Indian acquaintance.

"To tell you the truth, I really fear what might happen if and when Nehru dies," he said. "In my opinion, Krishna Menon is an evil man. He's hungry for power. For that very reason I doubt if he would invite the Communists to take over—even though he often seems to be in their corner. He knows that once they're in, the power center shifts.

But what I fear is that, through his control of the army, he could and would literally divide India.

"The trouble is that right now no one knows what the secret of his influence over Nehru really is. We just know it's a powerful one."

In 1962, the Chinese incursion into the Northeast Frontier would put an end to that influence. For the military was discovered to be in vast disarray. An aroused public literally forced Nehru to sack the man most responsible, Defense Minister Krishna Menon (who retired to Kerala to lick his wounds).

I had another concern. Nehru insisted that progress could only be made within a socialist framework. What he had seen of the unregulated capitalism of India had convinced him of its inherent rapacity.

"Small factories in the rural areas," he had said, "do help to lessen unemployment. But effective national progress can be made only if industry is engaged in a big way. It is important then to have basic industries. Such basic industries can only be owned by the state."

He actually authorized the establishment of fourteen training-cum-production institutes across the country. They were equipped with appropriate tools and machines and staffed by men who, by academic training and professed interest, could encourage would-be entrepreneurs. They were intended to bring into existence "small factories in the rural areas."

After these institutes had been in place for several years, I called on the earnest young man connected with them. "Frankly," he confided, "I'm discouraged. A survey team has just issued its report, and they had scarcely a good word to say. As it stands now, we just haven't been able to get off the ground."

But if the private sector was in a muddle, the public sector was in a mess. In April, 1963, the special correspondent to the *Christian Science Monitor*, Sharokh Sabavala, reported:

> India's government-owned Hindustan Steel, Ltd., showed a loss of 160,000,000 rupees ($33,600,000) in 1962. If depre-

ciation is added to this, the total loss incurred by the Indian taxpayer amounts to 400,000,000 rupees. . . . A recent audit, which showed the above, also described as "abnormal" the fact that raw materials worth 679,600,000 rupees ($142,716,000) at the three plants have not been accounted for. . . . Mention also is made that over 2,000,000 rupees ($420,000) advanced against the muster rolls has not been accounted for.

Apparently rapacity was not limited merely to Indian *capitalism*. Unfortunately, Hindustan Steel was not an isolated example.

Critics could cite many reasons for this sad state of affairs. But socialist leader Dr. Ram Manohar Lohia, addressing India's parliament, declared that the real root of the problem was the preoccupation of every Indian with promotion of the "interest of his own family, caste and community, by fair means or foul, and unfortunately no odium is attached to this pernicious habit."[1]

Neither capitalism nor socialism was likely to eradicate this pervasive problem. But it flourished best in an inoperative marketplace. Nevertheless, for many years to come, government leaders would find it politically expedient to assert their unswerving devotion to socialism.

There were, I discovered, more ways than one for the people at the top to wipe out the gains made by the people at the bottom. Even so, my hopes remained high. For Nehru's intentions—if not his policies—remained benevolent. He had been strongly influenced by Mahatma Gandhi. Gandhi had not only opened the path to independence by his program of nonviolent noncooperation, he had also insisted that the real value of any program for India was proven by what happened in her villages. Was this admonition still taken seriously?

*   *   *

Nehru's minister of health had been close to the Mahatma. I resolved to see her; perhaps she could give me some preview of the road ahead.

36

Raj Kumari Amrit Kaur: The name conjured up scenes of warriors, palaces, intrigue, and romance. Could she know much about villages? Well, birth control was her special province. Surely *that* was village related.

Frankly, I was surprised that a *woman* had been given such responsibility and authority. It didn't fit the picture that had been forming in my mind. For early on someone had told me, "Suppose you are driving on a country road. You go around a curve, and you see that the road is blocked by a woman and a cow. Hit the *woman*. The villagers might forgive you for that. They'd never forgive you if you hit the cow."

In the villages men ordered and dominated the women's lives. In fact, from the time she was a little girl, her father or brothers determined a woman's future life. Above all, they arranged her marriage—and she was required to conform to their wishes.

The duty was awesome. For according to Hindu mythology, the laws given by Manu, the father of all people, decreed, "A woman must be given in marriage before her breasts swell. And if she has menstruated before her marriage, both the giver and the taker fall into the abyss of hell; and her father, grandfather, and great-grandfather are born insects in ordure."

Of course, in these modern times, the sophisticated ignore such laws. In fact, the constitution of India forbids child marriage. But in many of the villages, the old "religious" sanctions remain strong. Even where religion has lost its suasion, custom still prevails. "This is the way our fathers did it. This is the way we do it."

In this complex land, where 80 percent of the people still lived in villages, women in high office were more prominent than in almost any other nation. Not only was Raj Kumari Amrit Kaur the minister of health, but Sucheta Kripalani was the chief minister of Uttar Pradesh; Mrs. T. V. Thomas was the food minister of Kerala; and in the ranks of the Congress Party, Nehru's daughter, Indira, was a major force to be reckoned with. In the next ten years, two hundred and fifty women would be called into senior civil-service positions. One would become prime minister.

So while the women of the lower castes continued to suffer the penalties prescribed by an ancient law, the women of the dominant castes scorned that law—even though its dogma insured their privileged status.

Caste, still observed (only untouchability was outlawed), provided India with its greatest burden—a burden that fell heaviest on the harijans and the village women.

But I had made an appointment with one who, as a Christian, did not observe caste, and as a close friend of Gandhi's, she had become a cabinet member in India's central government.

Toward the end of one of New Delhi's hottest days I took a cab out to the secretariat—that massive, impressive pile built by the British when they moved the capital from Calcutta. The British were gone and the multilayered bureaucracy of the government of India occupied its corridors and cubicles. Walking down the wide halls, I finally found Raj Kumari's office.

The interview was well worth the trip. For this wisp of energy and bright intelligence bubbled with ideas. Daughter of a prominent family (her brother was governor of Bombay State), she had served for sixteen years as Gandhi's "secretary in charge of English correspondence." Recognizing her virtues, Nehru had appointed her to his cabinet.

She immediately made me feel welcome, directing me to a wide, comfortable chair while she leaned back in her own. I asked about Gandhi.

"Gandhiji drove himself far more than most people knew," she said. "I once laughingly chided him, 'Now, you must not forget that the nonviolence you preach is also meant to apply to the treatment you give yourself.' "

"What did he say to that?" I asked.

"He barely smiled and went right on doing what he was doing."

Then we spoke of family planning.

"Oh, we're really working on that. In the next five-year plan there will be a substantial increase in appropriations for that very program."

I felt uncomfortable with that answer, remembering the conversation I had had in Calcutta with one impressive-looking Anglo-Indian.

"There doesn't seem to be as many cows on the street as when I was here three years ago," I remarked as I looked out the window of our bus. "Why is that?"

"Oh, they're moving them out—just as the five-year plan said they would. They're doing the same thing with the beggars."

"What do they do with the beggars?"

"Why, they put them in homes of some sort. They're doing the same thing with the prostitutes. In one month they gathered them all up—the whole bloody lot."

Had I not been besieged by a host of beggars and pimps as I left my hotel that morning, I might have believed him. He was one of many who reckoned that if a goal is stated in a five-year plan, it is—abracadabra—accomplished.

But Raj Kumari Amrit Kaur was no bumpkin. She was astute and articulate. "I believe you know, as Gandhi did, that continence is the method we really should urge," she continued.

"Yes, but realistically—"

"I know. We're not stopping there. Right now we are trying to find out all we can about the rhythm method. It's a 'natural' way. And the Catholic Church says it works.

"To help make it work, we're developing a system that uses colored beads. Doctors and midwives will determine a woman's menstrual cycle. Then the woman will wear the beads in such a way that, as she moves a bead each day, certain colored beads will appear and will indicate that she has arrived at her 'safe' period. We'll have to wait and see how it works."

Four years later they found that it *didn't* work. Men evidently ignored the system. Many women, especially in the villages, thought the beads were some sort of magic. Just move them to the right color and—voila!—you were safe.

When the interview came to an end, Raj Kumari walked with me to the door. Her parting words were admonitory: "John, never forget that there is plenty of friendship and fellow feeling in all the peoples of the world. The misunderstandings that divide man from man are caused wholly and solely by politicians. But alas, for good or evil, our destinies lie in their hands."

It was a treble echo of John Nuveen's earlier verdict. It didn't augur well for grass-roots democracy. Later I would wonder if they were both right. But, for now, I simply thanked her for her time and counsel and went on my way.

Of two things, however, I was sure. First, when it came to birth control, Gandhi—wise though he may have been—had left India ill-provisioned. Second, Gandhi had been on the mark when he insisted that the building of India should start in her villages.

In spite of the general decline of his influence, Gandhi has left to India—and to the world—more than a few wise, able, and dedicated disciples. One of them was a Christian pastor named Joseph John.

In 1946 Joseph had met the Mahatma, who had told him that—as far as he, Gandhi, was concerned—the essence of Christianity was expressed in Jesus' words, "I tell you, whatsoever you do for one of the least of these my brothers, you do for me"(*see* Matthew 25:40). The words had been burned into Joseph's heart.

In 1955, I met this Spirit-filled Gandhian Christian. He had once been the pastor of a growing, vital church. One day he had a visit from one of his parishioners, a farmer, who was in deep despair. The man's resources were gone; he didn't know where to turn. Joseph thought he knew the answer. It was in Paul's Letter to the Philippians (4:19).

"Don't forget," he told his parishioner, " 'My God shall supply all your need according to his riches in glory. . . .' God loves you. You believe that, don't you, Elisha?"

Elisha just looked at him for a while. Finally he spoke, "Pastor, you can say that sort of thing because you get a salary. I have to live on what comes out of the ground. How can I believe that God loves me when nothing has come out of it for the past two years? Look at me. I have no more seed to plant. I have nothing to put into the mouths of my children. You come and sit where I sit and let me hear you quote Scripture."

Deeply troubled, Joseph returned home, and for the next three days he sought God's will. Could he, from a position of privilege, continue to preach that God loved all men if he couldn't demonstrate its truth under the kind of conditions in which the farmer lived?

As Joseph prayed, he felt he heard God say, "Joseph, give up your church. Take your family. Go sit where the farmer sits. Don't worry. For I will be your security. And I will show Elisha, through you, that I love him."

To Joseph it was time for action. To hear from Gandhi was one thing. To hear from God was another.

The decision was not easy. It meant giving up a career that was bright with promise. It meant surrendering a position for which years of study had prepared him. But supported by a devoted wife and a small circle of dedicated friends, Joseph took his little family into the desolate area from which Elisha had come.

They were not well received. Most of the good land was owned by caste Hindus. Some met this young Christian minister with cynicism and hostility. Three times they burned the thatched buildings the family had erected; three times other Hindu neighbors helped them rebuild. Finally, digging with mattock and basket where no one believed water could be found, Joseph and his family struck what seemed an ever-flowing artesian spring.

It began a transformation. Once-hopeless people, many of them leprous, were now able to cultivate once-useless land, now laden with grain as irrigation brought it alive. A new community, with a new spirit, had come into being.

True, its outreach was limited, its resources minuscule. But it vividly demonstrated that God loved even the poorest of the poor—whose needs could be, and were being, supplied.

I heard about this new community, whose name meant "home of the friend of the poor." "If you really want to see how grass-roots community development works," said one of the more thoughtful missionaries, "you ought to go see this man, Joseph John." So one morning I started. Down the road through Ranipet and Sholapur, up the highway to Ramakrishnapet, then along miles of a meandering track. Finally I came to Deenabandupuram itself.

When our Land Rover rolled in, I was lovingly welcomed. I found myself in the midst of a thriving little complex: the clinic, the school, the orphanage, the smithy, the fields of rippling grain, the huge well. But what impressed me most were the people—happy, eager, energetic, self-reliant.

That evening, as we walked across the threshing floor, I shared my feelings. "Joseph, you've got something wonderful here. But it needs to spread."

"Yes, I know," he broke in. "And I've heard of you—and the fine way you're helping at Katpadi. I'm so glad for all of them there."

"Well, I was just going to ask you something. If we joined hands with you—found some additional personnel, some needed equipment—would you be willing to see how far this beginning can be extended? I must warn you, though, we could be aggravating partners."

I explained that we worked on a basis of mutual commitment, that our modest help would be available only for specific objectives and only for a limited period. We would expect to monitor developments and to receive periodic reports. If reports became delinquent, payments would cease.

He looked at me, silent for many minutes.

"I hope you'll understand me," he finally said. "I'd welcome such a relationship. But I want to make this reservation—don't push me into attempting more than I could do with local resources, in case you ever change your mind."

With that we shook hands, birthing a long-lasting, treasured relationship.

This meant, initially, a modest addition to the staff: some medical personnel, some agricultural equipment, a "social education" instructor, some visual aids, and some transport. More wells were dug, more pumps provided.

Before long a local cooperative was formed. Its members were Hindu, Christian, and Muslim. With them were lodged the major decisions. Carefully supervised credit was arranged for. An expanded crafts program was begun. The project began to really move.

As the years increased, so did the program. A small hospital came into being. Teams of local young people, called "peace armies," went from village to village, demonstrating new methods, inspiring, instructing, and organizing. Sales offices were established in the nearby towns, providing outlets for the expanding crafts and village industries.

Not every effort succeeded. We were not magicians. But we tried not to be fools (who "rush in where angels fear to tread"). We recognized that not every need was also a valid opportunity.

One need existed in a village Joseph and I visited after several years of working together. I had never met a more helpless, disheartened, apathetic aggregation of humanity. Caught in a system they could neither change nor escape, the people had given up. They had been crucified by circumstance, and they despaired of resurrection.

Most of the villagers had gone into debt—to get their daughters married, to buy new seed, to tide their families over a bad-crop year. The ruinous interest had increased, until now the moneylenders' agents were taking 80 percent of their crops as past-due payments on their mounting debts. The villagers, in turn, had become unwilling to work harder and risk more, when their part of the prospective increase would be so little. They were hungry, helpless, and hopeless.

Their well had collapsed. They asked for our help on their immediate problem. We gave it.

"But Joseph," I ventured, "this doesn't really solve their problem. They're still head-over-heels in debt."

"How would you feel," he answered, "about putting some of this year's appropriation into a revolving-loan program? I could make sure the loans were properly used. At least some of these people could get out of debt."

"Sounds good to me," I replied. "Let's try it."

We began with a small number who were deemed most credit worthy. When those few had paid back their loans, funds then became available to others.

It took us five years to get that village out of debt. At the end of that time, I visited with them again. The difference was like night and day. Where they had once been apathetic and crushed, they were now energetic and eager. Nine of the farmers had gone together and dug a huge irrigation well. Because there were so many of them, they could afford a power-driven pump. All their fields were now irrigated. The village was alive and moving—clean, prosperous, and self-sufficient.

With Joseph, I walked through it. Mothers, in new and neat dresses, stood in the doorways and thanked us. Bright-eyed children danced beside us. Fathers proudly led us to the huge jars of stored grain. Gratitude bubbled up inside me—that we, with such modest resources, had made such a major difference.

Finally, we had, I thought, seen it all. Gratified, I moved toward our transport. But wait! They had one more thing to show me. With high expectancy, they led me toward the banyan tree in the center of the village. A few men, oblivious to the harsh rays of the midday sun, began to dig in what seemed a sort of grave. As layer after sandy layer was removed, I finally saw it—a phallic symbol, the village idol.

"This," said the headman, "was our god; the only god we ever knew, the god of our fathers. But," he continued as he again covered the stone lingam with dirt, "we now want to find out about your God—the God who makes you do what you have done for us. We want to become Christians."

No effort had been made to proselytize. It had been made clear to them that our help was theirs with no strings attached.

But love is its own evangel, and they would not be denied. So the Church of South India extended its pastoral care to this village. Three years later I came back to worship with them in their little mud-brick sanctuary. Even later, I returned to help dedicate their granite-block church—one of the first of more than a score of such churches up and down the valley, built not with funds from some foreign-missions board but proudly and happily by the villagers themselves.

I have returned many times to meet the people of these expanding villages. At first I knew them as outcasts, lepers, half-naked owners of nothing—the serfs and chattels of those who lorded over them. Now they come by proudly, fully clothed, heads erect, and eyes shining. For now they have land, grow food, make money, and read books. They have built homes and schools and clinics and churches.

On one occasion I went out to a new area to watch as a group dug their wells and prepared their land. Deciding to try to help a little, I went down the steep steps hewn out of the clay sides of the well, placed a basket full of the newly excavated dirt on my head, and went back up the steps to dump it. It had looked so easy for the women, whose task this was, but I soon discovered that nearly any of them could out carry, out climb, and out last me under the hot tropical sun. So I retired to the shade of a thatched-roof shed.

After a while the headman of the new group—with several of his associates—joined me. He wanted to know once more just who we were and what made us do what none had done before. I took the time to tell him.

When I had finished, he rose to his feet, brushing the dirt from his ragged clothes. He looked like a brigand—perhaps he had been. But now his face glowed.

"Do you see these eyes?" he said. "These hands? These feet? They're yours!"

He stood for a moment longer, hands outstretched. Then he sat down. The air was alive with something too meaningful for words. I reached for his right hand, held it for a moment, and swallowed something that seemed to have lodged in my throat. Then we went back to work.

The movement goes on, extending its impact and spreading its influence. Although Joseph John gives us great credit, we are only one of many agencies helping its many facets to expand. But that help is steadily diminishing. For the major support comes from its own self-generating resources.

Best of all, the work begun by Joseph is now being directed and extended by Joseph's children—whom I have seen grow from callow youths into self-assured adults.

One of the more significant aspects has been the development of a program for the delivery of health care to the rural poor. Medical doctors Premchander and Harikumari John contend that hospital care, necessary as it may be in some critical cases, is mostly available to the urban or more privileged classes. The truly rural poor—with incomes that average about eight cents a day—can afford neither the time nor the funds to leave their fields and animals and make the long and costly trip to the hospital. Even "mobile units" can provide only sporadic and inadequate attention—most of it curative rather than preventive.

The answers, they discovered, lay in the villages themselves. But this required reevaluation and readjustment. First of all, they were forced to divest themselves of their "elite" preconceptions. They were typically Western in believing that well-trained professionals were essential to any health program's success, that village-level workers—without constant supervision—were incapable of wise analysis and appropriate procedures, that "approved" systems had to be imposed, that Western procedures must displace indigenous practices, that costly drug medication was always superior to readily available herbal remedies, and that the problems of the poor were self-imposed. They early recognized the inseparable relationship between prevailing health and existing socioeconomic structure. They came to see that, to succeed, a program must be desired and designed by the entire village, not merely its "leaders."

Slowly disengaging themselves from curative medicine, these dedicated doctors now spend the bulk of their time enlarging a corps of village health workers. Most of these are mature women of thirty-five to forty years of age (many of whom were village midwives) whom they carefully and recurrently train. Over 80 percent of the preliminary health care of the villages is now taken care of by the village health workers.

To the new training center at Madras now come "students" from across India, Bangladesh, Malaysia, and West Germany. It is a potent, pervasive enterprise.

And in the seventy-eight villages around Deenabandu, results have been almost startling. As health has constantly improved, infant mortality has steadily declined. As infant mortality has declined and as the villagers see their children stay well and grow strong, they become more than ready to listen to the message of family planning. Deenabandu therefore enjoys the reputation of being among the first, and perhaps the foremost in rural India, to win and hold acceptors, whose contraceptive regimen is routinely administered by the village health workers. It was the earliest, and for a considerable time the only, center in India to administer Depo-

Provera (an antipregnancy injection given once every three months and approved by authorities in more than sixty nations).

Under careful supervision of doctors, the family-planning program has been safe, widely accepted, and constantly growing. More than a third of child-bearing women in the area now practice birth control.

So the "mustard seed" of a love that extended concern and demanded responsibility has become a "mighty tree." We, alongside many others, have helped to nourish it. Today its branches encompass the whole gamut of community development. Chandran and Hari's work has been augmented by the rich contribution of their brother, Karuna, who has a degree in agriculture, and their sister, Gita, who has a degree in nutrition. Hundreds of indigenous village leaders have also become ardent "trainers of trainers."

Out of this project has come the realization that development is not a "product" extruded by some superior agency. For real development is an inside job—an evolution, not an importation, a growth, not a gift. It is evolved, not conferred, and comes from modest affiliation, not massive intervention. It results from a synergism between expatriate help and indigenous competence. The operation at Deenabandu has been such a synergism.

Still, at one time I concluded we were probably irrelevant. The government of India's second five-year plan included a provision for the establishment of a ministry of community development. Sushil K. Dey was named to head it up, and workers for the program were enlisted. Block development officers—each responsible for from fifty to one hundred villages—were trained in administration. A small army of "experts"—in agriculture, village cooperatives, and related disciplines—were enrolled to serve under them. The Bharat Sevak Samaj was assigned the task of inspiring local volunteers. When the government of India proclaimed the program ready to transform all her 500,000 villages, I asked for an appointment with S. K. Dey.

This stocky, intelligent, blunt, and tired man received me in his office at the secretariat.

I came straight to the point: "Mr. Minister, I'm here to see whether we should remain in India. You've announced that your program will soon involve all of India's villages. So what would be the point in a small group like ours trying to do with so little what you can do with so much? To put it in a nutshell, haven't we become redundant? Wouldn't we actually be in the way?"

He pushed back his chair and looked out across the city. "Listen, Mr. Peters, we've taken on an enormous task. Maybe someday we'll reach all our villages. But as of now, I can tell you we're in trouble.

"Part of our problem is that we really don't have any sociologists in India. Oh, we've got people back from England and America, with degrees in sociology. But what do the textbook writers of England and America know about India—especially village India?"

He had put his finger squarely on one of the government's major problems—an educational system almost completely unrelated to Indian reality.

"You see," he said, "we not only have to deal with almost one-sixth of the world's people, we have to decide what to do with one-fourth of the world's cattle. And we face attitudes and taboos that almost preclude a solution."

I knew what he was talking about—scrawny herds roved the countryside, independent foragers, neither cared for nor interfered with. One almost forgot that much of what they devoured might have been eaten by the hungry denizens of the swarming bustees.

It was, I had to admit, not so everywhere. In Mysore, for instance, I had suddenly come upon a cow with a totally adequate udder. It was so unusual that, for a moment, I felt acutely embarrassed.

But S. K. Dey continued: "Now let me deal with your original question. Of *course* you're not 'in the way,' as you say. There will always be a place for pioneering efforts like yours. You have some real advantages, you see. You can undertake methods and approaches that government, with its cumbersome machinery, finds difficult if not impossible. Then, when the validity of these new approaches has been demonstrated, government can standardize and multiply them."

I thanked this thoughtful, hard-working minister and left. I felt relieved that he thought there was a place for us. But I questioned his assumption that government could "standardize and multiply" what others had developed. Could love and concern and sensitivity be made "government issue"? I doubted it.

In other ways, S. K. Dey was an accurate prophet—he *was* in trouble. As time passed his community-development program came under increasing criticism from those who expected too much too soon. In spite of a huge increase in appropriations, the accomplishments of the program fell far below its stated goals. It seemed impossible to move the initiative from the placid bureaucrats to the passive people. The Bharat Sevak Samaj sadly concluded, "No government agency can inspire the masses."

No one mentioned a factor that, after Gandhi, was almost wholly lacking from the program—a *spiritual* commitment. The stress was on technical competence, which was rarely attained, and on prospective advancement, which was a probability only to those with the right connections.

On a short train ride from Poona to Bombay I learned how unlikely spiritual commitment was. My seatmate, a distinguished consultant, discovered why I was in India. As he listened to my description of our plans, I could sense his barely concealed skepticism. When I finished, he turned to me with a half smile. "Now tell me, what is the *real* reason—the honest motivation—for your work?"

I half smiled back. "Well, you'll probably not believe me, but— while motivation is almost always mixed—I'd say that the basic reason for our program is love."

His eyebrows shot up. He looked startled, embarrassed. "That means religion, I suppose?"

"Yes, I suppose it does."

"Frankly," he said, "I'm not a religious man. And I can't see religion as an answer to our problems. Look at what it has done for India—the divisions, the injustices, the cruelties it has spawned.

"Take our Emperor Aurangzeb," he continued, warming to his subject. "He had only four wives, when he could have had hundreds. He hated dancing girls. He never drank. He went to prayers faithfully and lived like a Spartan. But how did he *become* emperor? By murdering his two brothers and throwing his old father, Shah Jahan, into prison for life! He killed and slew 'infidels' by the thousand. He was one of the most religious of men—and one of the cruelest."

He sat back, glowering triumphantly.

Our journey was approaching its end.

"Let's be happy we didn't live in his time," I murmured, remembering that we *had* lived in the times of Hitler and Stalin—men who were not particularly religious. "But I would speculate that a lust for power, not a hunger for religion, turned a man like Aurangzeb into a monster. . . . All I know is that if we're to stay with this huge, dirty job of shaping the world into something fine and decent, nothing less than love is a sufficient motive. And a life motivated by love is really a life transformed by religion in its best sense."

I let it go at that. But I had no confidence that my words had convinced him.

About this time, I had what seemed an inspired idea. I would bring together a national board of World Neighbors, made up of India's most reputable leaders. Where better to begin than with vice-president Sarvepalli Radhakrishnan?

For this esteemed political leader who would become India's president had also served in the United Nations, been a professor at Oxford, and was widely known as a philosopher and author. I had, I must confess, read only enough of his works to realize that—in spite of some very real differences—we shared common interests in our appreciation for the mystical and our concern for brotherhood.

"Truly religious souls," he had said in his Beatty Memorial Lectures, at McGill University, "will identify themselves with the social and human revolution that is afoot and guide the aspirations of mankind for a better and fuller life. . . . Peace is not the mere absence of war; it is the development of a strong fellow-feeling, an honest appreciation of other people's ideas and values."[2]

That didn't really equal the Sermon on the Mount, but it bolstered my audacity. So I called his office and, amazingly, was invited to meet the vice-president for tea just two days later.

When I gave my destination to the tall Sikh whose taxi pulled up to the door of my small hotel that afternoon, his face took on a new expression. When we arrived at the vice-president's home, he waited—wondering, I suppose, if I'd actually be received.

The immaculately groomed servant who met me at the door led me into a small, pleasantly shaded salon just off the entryway. In seconds, Dr. Radhakrishnan, clothed in cool, traditional white, strolled in, casually wiping his wire-rimmed glasses. He extended his hand, Western style, in a hearty greeting.

After ordering up tea, he asked me to be seated. He immediately wanted to know about our work and movement. I gave him the story from the beginning—mentioning my hope for a national board in India and hastening to ask him if he would consider its chairmanship.

He paused. A slow smile gathered on his face as he said, "You must know that what you are doing—this bringing together of men of different races and creeds in a common enterprise—is at the very center of my heart's concern. But I must remind you, and myself, that as vice-president of a nation such as India, I have duties that occupy my full time. Frankly," he chuckled, "I'm afraid that I don't think of this as often as I need to."

He mentioned the many speaking engagements and other assignments he had already accepted in various parts of the world. "Far too many," he said.

I rose to go. He joined me, and we walked to the door. His servant had already called a cab.

"I do appreciate your asking me," he said in parting. "And I'm sure you see why I cannot accept. Come again when you're in New Delhi."

Within a few days the fever for top-level representation had left me, departing as suddenly as it attacked. During one cool dawn I once again recognized that ours was a "percolate up," not a "trickle down" system.

So putting aside any idea of a national board, I headed for the villages. I needed to examine the progress of some of our assisted projects.

Leaving Uttar Pradesh, I made my way by train and Jeep to Damoh, a railhead city in Madhya Pradesh. There, in "tiger country," World Neighbors was helping Peter Solomon expand an exciting community-development effort. A whirlwind tour of village projects followed, with receptions almost everywhere.

But the most impressive was an outdoor high tea on the eve of my departure. Project leaders and city officials were all there. As the affair moved toward its conclusion, one suddenly asked me—in a voice that reached all corners of the lawn—"Dr. Peters, what about Little Rock?"

This was 1960. Less than three years earlier, Governor Orval Faubus had called out the Arkansas National Guard, ostensibly to "keep order," but actually to block the federally ordered integration of Little Rock's Central High School. President Dwight Eisenhower, in turn, had sent in the army, and the "integration" proceeded—but not without ugly incident.

I *knew* about Little Rock, having grown up there and graduated from its excellent but segregated high school. I had left there at eighteen and gone to Oklahoma.

All this time I had learned from my relatives and friends that times were changing in Little Rock. Two of those relatives were teachers in the local school system—and risked livelihood and reputation by openly opposing Governor Faubus's rearguard action.

I had, in fact, come back to Little Rock, to visit my mother and father, only a few hours after the convulsive eruption that marred the attempted enrollment of black students. By the time I arrived, the first spasm of bigotry had begun to subside. But reporters—national and international—still crowded the streets and coffee shops around Central High. In a drugstore on Sixteenth Street, just off the campus, I found a younger cousin of mine—a photographer for Associated Press. He was nursing a cold cup of coffee and seemed completely unsurprised at my appearance.

I drew up a chair. "Ferd, what's going on?"

"Almost nothing. That's our problem. We're being bombarded by telegrams to 'get some action pictures.' But for now, things are just too calm."

For the 101st Airborne now surrounded the area. A few days earlier, one of their number, keeping order, had lowered his bayoneted rifle. His complexion was a bit darker than that of his fellows, and his action was immediately photographed. The picture was flung across the country by the national press—an angry black coercing the local whites. He was, in fact, Hawaiian.

One smart young high school student, sensing the hunger for news, brought over a roll of film. It was, he said, a roll he shot of the black students being seated in class. He offered it to the highest bidder. The newsman who secured the much-wanted roll with a bid of $200 found that it was blank.

Suddenly there was a shout, "Come on. Here's something."

We all rushed out.

From around the corner filed a scrawny, bedraggled procession. Eight teenagers, their faces emptied of intelligence or purpose, carried crude, hastily made signs that read: GO HOME, NIGGER. GO BACK WHERE YOU BELONG. KEEP OUR SCHOOLS WHITE!

It was a media gimmick, conceived and paid for by some reporter. *How typical*, I wondered, *is this sort of thing?* The eight kids marched back and forth until the photographers were sated.

This retinue of pictures—first the contorted faces of the hate-filled bigots, then the contrived "threats" of the soldiers, and finally the arranged "protests" of the teenagers—had preceded me and penetrated even into the jungle-enveloped villages of central India. Now I was being introduced to a question intended to deflate and embarrass any American.

I thought long and hard. Somehow, ashamed and dismayed as I was of what had happened, I didn't feel inclined to grovel. I had seen and heard too many of my peers—especially in the arts, religion, and academe—court the approbation of their critical hosts by expressing a near-loathing of America and what went on there. I had been abroad long enough to know that similar things "went on" almost everywhere. But things *had* gone wrong in Little Rock.

"I don't know what you have read in your newspapers," I finally said to a crowd grown suddenly silent. "It may be true, and I am sorry. I only want to remind you that what is true of one area may not be typical of the country as a whole. In fact, newspapers report things not because they are normal but because they are *news*.

"Just recently, for instance, I read in the *Times of India* where three harijans decided to enter a temple at Gorakhpur to worship— as was their right under your constitution. The Brahman priest made them welcome—as was his duty. But this so infuriated some of the community that a mob descended on the temple, murdered the harijans and the priest, and burned their bodies in the village square.

"I've read many other stories—almost as bad as this one. But if I said, after reading them, 'Well, that's India,' you would know I was unfair. For the stories were in the papers because they were *not* what's happening everywhere. They were there because they were unusual. That's what made them *news*.

"Now, the United States and India have more in common than

some of us may realize. We are both democracies. We both won our independence from the British. And we both have deep and serious problems.

"*Our* problem just now is the problem of segregation. It has its roots in the vile custom of slavery. Slavery, of course, has been abolished, and segregation has been declared unconstitutional. But many communities still cling to old patterns and still resist new relationships.

"*Your* problem, on the other hand, is the problem of untouchability. It's rooted in your caste system, which makes it more difficult than ever to deal with. Even though it's been ruled out in your constitution and denounced in your courts, you know and I know that it is still widely observed, especially in your villages.

"Actually, of course, we're not talking just about *national* problems. We're talking about *human* problems. They're ages old and deeply ingrained. The clashes between tribes and castes and colors and creeds happen not just in the United States and in India; they happen in the new African states, in Northern Ireland, in Malaysia, in fact, almost everywhere.

"In America we now know that these attitudes are wrong. We're trying to change. As a matter of fact, the events in Little Rock, bad as they were, happened because some people—black and white— were trying to change a no-longer-tolerable system.

"So you're going to have to be patient with us. And we're going to have to be patient with you. Maybe one day we'll discover how closely akin to each other we actually are."

Long before I finished, they were wagging their heads in assent. When I said good-bye, I felt I was leaving real friends, real brothers and sisters. Even the man who asked the question had become cordial.

But I wasn't really at ease with what I had said. First of all, I wasn't black. So how could I know what the Little Rock experience had meant to those most directly affected? I could try, but I knew it wasn't enough.

I sat on top of a pile of manure while the high-wheeled cart on which it was loaded lurched drunkenly toward the old town of Ahmadnagar. The dry, white dust rose in drifting, lazy plumes from the hooves of the plodding oxen, to settle back, like suffocating caresses, on every tiny orifice of nostril, skin, and fabric. I was miserable. The malodorous "cushion" on which I sat was my only creature comfort. *Will I ever reach my destination?* I wondered.

The journey had begun auspiciously enough. The previous evening, in Bombay's vast and raucous Victoria Station, I had found my train and compartment with no difficulty. But the schedule was, for me, impossible to read. So I said to a guard as I clambered aboard, "When do we get to Ahmadnagar?" I was to be met there by friends and taken on some thirty miles, by Jeep, to Vadala, the project I intended to visit.

"At ten in the morning," the guard replied. I relaxed.

All night the train climbed smoothly and steadily through the lofty Western Ghats. Around 7:30, it pulled into a neat little station. I wondered as I sat, bag unpacked and half undressed, where we were. Too late, as we pulled away, I saw the sign at the end of the station platform. AHMADNAGAR, it read.

Eighteen miles later the train paused. I leaped off, and the train pulled away.

At the minuscule station, sitting almost alone on the high, desolate plain, I learned the returning train would pass through that evening at 8:00 P.M. There was no other transportation—no truck, no car, no taxi, only the stationmaster's bicycle. I was desperate. This could throw my whole schedule into shambles. Sitting on my bag, I wished for a miracle.

Finally, a bullock cart lumbered down the road. A young farmer was bound somewhere with a load of manure. For four rupees, I persuaded him to add me to that load and take me back to Ahmadnagar. We reached there in the early afternoon, stopping at the railway station. My friends had long since given me up and returned to Vadala.

When I could get enough dust out of my throat to talk, I asked the station agent where I might find accommodations.

"You might try Ahmadnagar College," he said. "They're used to foreign visitors."

They obviously were. For Principal Tom Barnabas made me welcome, despite my barnyard redolence.

The twelve-year-old college had been founded by a remarkable Indian Christian, Dr. B. P. Hivale. His purpose, he had said, was to give rural boys an opportunity for an education so that they would provide leadership in the uplifting of their people.

It was a worthy purpose, and I was excited at its prospect. For I felt certain that, if India were to succeed in her vast struggle to feed, clothe, house, and educate her people, she would certainly need the serious and sacrificial involvement of her academic community in the problems of her rural areas. I knew most of India's people lived in the village and off the land. Ideally, her educational institutions could be reservoirs of leadership and uplift. Here was a college with an intention of becoming such a reservoir. I began to feel my ride on the bullock cart had been no accident.

"How many of your graduates are back in the village?" I asked.

The question almost answered itself. For young men in India seek education to escape, not reshape, the village. With their parents' full approval, they flock to the cities, hoping to find jobs and perhaps send back a rupee or two to families who would otherwise never see such largesse.

Dr. Barnabas could name almost no graduates who had returned. Both of us, considering the implications, became deeply troubled. For we knew something had gone wrong if a system that intended to uplift an area actually lured away its most promising leadership. The kind of education that produced self-conscious sophisticates, weaned from drudgery and scornful of labor, was something no developing nation could afford.

In part of our long discussion, I proposed that we would provide support for a village-oriented program that combined research and service. The village, not the campus, would be focus and laboratory.

Dr. Barnabas felt sure any course that required college students to "work like coolies in the dirt of the villages" would never receive accreditation. I, on the other hand, was certain the college could not find a professor who had what it took to successfully direct such a program—enough sensitivity to be accepted by villagers, enough dedication to labor with harijans, enough inspiration to cause students to emulate him.

We were both wrong. I was the first to be proved so.

Even while I sat looking out over the high plains of Maharashtra, S. K. Hulbe was half a world away. Once an orphaned lad in an Indian village, he had been adopted by a loving missionary. Now he was studying at the University of Texas, "working like a coolie" on his PhD. Hulbe was on leave from Ahmadnagar College! When I returned to the United States, I went to see him.

In his small apartment in Austin, we hammered out the outlines of an operating program, agreed upon a tentative budget, and made mutual commitments: When the classwork for his doctorate was completed, Hulbe would return to Ahmadnagar. With our help he would begin a pioneering, creative experiment in college-village cooperation.

Once I heard that the new project was actually underway, I could just see the whole thing in my mind's eye—the happy villagers welcoming those who had come at last to deliver them from their age-old miseries, the garlands, the greetings, the homage. Perhaps Dr. Hulbe and his first student contingent anticipated the same. The project, in any event, was launched with high hopes.

Its reception, however, became a disaster. The villagers, tired "of social workers who come out to preach to us," made it abundantly clear they did not welcome this collegiate "invasion." Government officials viewed the effort with jaundiced eyes. The wider academic community appeared scandalized at a proposal in which college students and faculty were compromised and contaminated by the heat and dust of the villages.

All this was a blow to me and a mountainous challenge to Hulbe's hopes and dreams. But Hulbe and his associates persisted, and our support and encouragement continued. Carefully evading the trap of mere "social work," the courses met high scholastic standards. They fulfilled a three-fold purpose: to reach and involve villagers—even the harijans—in programs of sound improvement; to so involve college students in village life that it would supply India's nation-building program with a growing cadre of competent and dedicated leadership at the grass-roots level; to make education more substantive and relevant by supplying valid data concerning the economic, social, and political life of India's rural society.

During its first few years, the project battled for its very life. Rural apathy and official vacillation almost choked it. Village factionalism and failing monsoons almost derailed it. Open opposition and covert suspicion all but stopped it. For this was an area where the Opposition [Communist] Party was strong. Had any United States government money been involved in its support, the project could never have survived.

But as the months passed, students, faculty, landowners, and harijans joined forces to build roads, erect buildings, terrace fields, try out new seeds, test soil, and organize cooperatives.

When news of all this reached me—through reports from the project and from the overseas staff we were beginning to establish—I readily and happily conceded that I had been so wrong. There *were* professors willing to swim against the current of custom, to forego the approval of their peers, to put aside personal aggrandizement. Hulbe and his fellows had proved it.

Within six years the project included a one-year, postgraduate diploma course in social work. It had a distinctly rural bias, and because it was actively involved with rural life and problems, it offered unique opportunities for field training and experience. The course was so successful that, seven years later, Poona University—under whose academic supervision the college program operated—upgraded it to a master's degree course, the only one at that time in the country.

Finally, when the central government's commission endorsed the program, colleges from across India began sending professors for orientation and training. As a result more than sixty other colleges incorporated comparable studies into their curricula, and the program at Ahmadnagar was recommended as a model for India's national-service scheme.

As the project demonstrated its value, other agencies also came forward to assist in its support. Besides the United Church's Board of World Ministries, these also included India's central and state governments, the University Grants Commission, the Planning Commission, and India's Council of Churches.[3]

In sum, the income of local farmers has doubled and trebled. In a district-wide review, the state of Maharashtra awarded "first prize in family planning" to the *taluk* (132 villages) that constituted the operational area of the program. It was no accident. For the college program had been the first in that area to introduce visual aids on family planning and the first to promote "vasectomy camps," where doctors gathered to perform the operation on large groups of men, in the villages themselves.

In India, any success in family planning is a cause for celebration.

If any area needed family planning it was Kerala—that lush, crowded state on India's southwestern coast, once called Travancore and Cochin. Though it resembled a tropical paradise, Kerala produced only a third of her food requirements. Her per capita income was around eleven cents a day. Though she had one of the highest literacy rates in India, her college graduates could not find jobs. She was the kind of "troubled water" in which the Communists loved to fish. They, more than anyone else, had prospered.

One prominent churchman urged us to extend our program to Kerala. "It's exactly what we need," he declared.

After I visited him, this dynamic man called together an assembly of leaders representing the numerous churches throughout central Kerala.

Soon after we began, one of them broached the crucial question: "How much money do you plan to bring into Kerala?"

"That all depends. How much investment do *you* plan to make? Because, really, this is *your* problem, isn't it? We all know, don't we, that the Communists are making progress in Kerala principally because the people face such a hopeless future. If they win, you and your people will be among the first to suffer. Now, we're willing to help if we can—though I must tell you that our resources are very limited. But the churches you represent must make the first move. I'm here to find out what programs, if any, you are intending to put into effect."

From that point on, the meeting deteriorated. There *were* no plans, because they had only looked forward to the money. We all went our separate ways. Conditions in the countryside worsened. The Communists won the state elections. Kerala's door seemed to have slammed shut.

Later, with my new aides Merlin and Eunice Bishop, we tried again and found concerned and involved leaders.

The best of these was K. Janardanan Pillai, secretary of the Kerala Gandhi Smarak Nidhi (Gandhi Memorial Association). In this organization—composed of Hindus, Christians, and Muslims— Gandhi's life and teachings were alive and relevant. Pillai had been inspired to give up a prestigious career, and his wife had foregone a place as a member of a wealthy Indian family to devote their lives to the needs of "the least of these, my brethren."

When Pillai heard us tell of World Neighbors, he simply asked, "What can we offer you that will help you fulfill your dream?"

The Gandhi Smarak Nidhi could offer a lot. Working on a shoestring, but with an extraordinary fund of dedication, they had established more than sixty centers throughout crowded, needy Kerala. Their goals were simple and direct: the improvement of every aspect of the lives of desperate villagers.

Being Gandhian, they had some reservations about birth control. But being realists, they added to community development an intensive educational program that encouraged family planning. Thus began a joint project that would ultimately reach and improve the lives of some 2 million people in various sectors of India's "problem state."

However, we found the achievements of our small, modestly funded voluntary program soon swallowed up in the profusion of publicity given to large, richly endowed governmental programs. Kerala had a plethora of block development officers, authorized to "double and treble" production. Various media spelled out the governmental goals in elaborate detail, even though their results were mired in bureaucratic limbo.

Merlin and I discussed this problem at great length. Finally Merlin asked Janardanan Pillai, "Can we actually double food production in Kerala? If so, could we put on a demonstration that couldn't be ignored?"

"Well," softly answered Mr. Pillai, "it has to be done. And if it should be done, it can be done."

So began the Trivandrum District Development Programme. We chose this location because it surrounded the very habitat of Kerala's state government. It began small: five pilot units comprising 200 acres of paddy, 10 acres of vegetables, and 200 kitchen gardens. It involved a farmer's institute for the intensive training of the hundreds of cultivators who would later be involved. It established a land army, consisting of young volunteers who would carry the message of "more and better food" to every household. It set up work camps to intensify concern for the satisfaction of basic needs.

Preceded by as big a propaganda campaign as we could marshal, the program took root and grew. Professors from the agricultural college were enlisted. New strains of rice were planted. Irrigation canals, like life-giving arteries, reached out across the laterite soil. Multiple cropping became commonplace. Yields doubled and trebled. Within three years 4,298 farmers participated. The state took notice.

At a dinner in Trivandrum I was given a seat between the minister of agriculture and Mr. Pillai. As we waited for dessert, the minister leaned across me. "I don't believe you've seen the evening paper, Janardanan, but we've announced that the state is now extending your program to forty blocks of Kerala." A "block" is an area about sixty miles square, which includes some sixty thousand farmers.

Mr. Pillai smiled and nodded. It meant that where we had only reached slightly more than four thousand farmers, the state had the potential of reaching more than 2 million. S. K. Dey's prophecy seemed to be coming true. Perhaps the government *could* "standardize and multiply" programs developed by voluntary agencies. I hoped so.

At any rate, when— a few years later—the central government of India drew up its Small Farmer's Development Agency and established it in sixteen separate states, it chose as its pattern the program born in Kerala.

The Trivandrum District Development Programme had begun in 1966. Because it had inoculated thousands of children and stressed the need for improved nutrition, it had drastically reduced the deaths of babies and young children. Some criticized such a program.

"You're only compounding India's basic problem—overpopulation," they said.

But in the *New York Times*, veteran correspondent Bernard Weinraub answered these critics:

> Over the past decade the birth rate in Kerala has fallen from 37 to 27 [per 1,000] or less. Over the last 20 years, however, India's birth rate has fallen from 41 to 37.2 per thousand. . . . Economists attribute this to several key factors: the death rate is nine per thousand and life expectancy may be as high as 60 years, placing Kerala on a par with European nations. *Because of low infant mortality and [increased] life expectancy*, couples tacitly acknowledge that their children will survive and that there is no pressure to have extra infants.[4]

Children, of course, are the only "social security" known to most of the world's poor. Because so many of these children die before maturity, parents feel required to have extra infants. Now, with the coming of increased income and lowered infant mortality, that pressure had been lifted. This meant the people of Kerala had 200,000 fewer births per year than did groups of comparable size throughout India.

Obviously, many factors conspired to bring about these results. Kerala's high degree of literacy, the valiant efforts of state and district officials, the yeoman work of the Kerala Family Planning Association were major influences. But the effective change agents must include those deeply motivated individuals who were inspired, assisted, and equipped to help their brothers and sisters.

Even so, though the strength of Communism appeared to be eroding, it continued its intermittent revivals in Kerala. I wondered why. For, while Christians represent about 3 percent of the Indian population, in Kerala they represent close to 30 percent. Kerala, in other words, is India's most Christian and most literate state. Yet it regularly elected avowed Communists to state and national office.

This troubled me. I sought the answer from T. C. N. Menon, the Communist member of the Indian Parliament from Kerala. He was back home in Ernakulam and graciously granted me an interview.

During World War II, Menon told me, he had served in the Indian Air Force, had resented the treatment he received from his American peers, had begun to read Marx, and in time had become an active Communist. "It satisfies me intellectually and spiritually," he said.

Now he listened to my troubled questions. "Mr. Menon, how does it happen that you, a Communist, are elected year after year from the district that has the heaviest concentration of Christians—in a state that has the greatest *number* of Christians—in all India?"

Mr. Menon chuckled. "Well, you see, when people become Christians in India, they do so because they feel they're going to have a better life. This is what they understand the Gospel—the 'Good News' the preacher brought them—to be saying.

"When they find this is not so, at least in this life, they become disillusioned. At this point we introduce them to Communism. We explain that the preachers were right in telling them that it is not God's will that men be forever tied to the wheel of karma, that Hinduism, like all religions, is a snare and a burden. 'Christians are right,' we say, 'when they tell you there can be a better life. They just forget to show you how to get there. So now we Communists will do that.'

"Mr. Peters, I don't care what the minister or the priest says on Sunday morning. I'm a labor leader. When I'm home, I'm meeting with these people seven days a week. They know I'll fight their battles for them, whether they be Protestants or Catholics—who usually vote as a bloc.

"In fact," he ended with a laugh, "we couldn't elect a single Communist to the Parliament without the Christian vote."

This shook me. Here this Communist was illustrating better than most theological seminary professors our very real failure in the presentation of the Christian message to so much of the hungry world. But I thought I might puncture his almost overweening cockiness, so I mentioned the losses his party had suffered in the last state election.

He shrugged. "We just didn't realize how fully the opposition would unite. We won the previous election with a plurality of twenty-six percent. We lost this last one with thirty-four percent. The election reflected shrewd politics, not public repudiation. We've learned our lesson. Next time we'll win."

"Do you think that ultimately the Communists will conquer state power, as Marx said they must, in all the dominant countries of the world?"

"Of course. It's inevitable."

"Would you resort to nuclear arms to bring it about?"

"That's not a relevant question. We won't have to."

We shook hands in parting. I couldn't help but like him. But I knew that, by the dicta of class warfare, he had to regard me as a sworn enemy.

Which of us would win? Which would *really* provide an answer to the Third World's hopes and dreams?

It has been nearly four decades since I first set foot on the tarmac at Palam Airport. During those years I have had a small part in the vast changes that have come to India. They came slowly. For dreams of a socialist utopia do not die swiftly or gracefully. But, around 1980, the pace of change quickened. In that year the net losses by India's nationalized industry were nearly five times the amount lost the year before.[5] Unfortunately, in Third World systems, those losses could be made up in only two ways: by wringing capital from the already impoverished or by accepting a burden of debt whose servicing would inhibit badly needed basic development. India was bleeding at an artery.

To aggravate the situation, the Soviet Union—defender and champion of international Communism—had invaded Afghanistan. Old relationships became more difficult to sustain. Old practices were more difficult to defend. So despite what seemed a growing distance between United States and Indian political postures, mainly over Pakistan, a real economic rapprochement began. Productivity in the private sector was encouraged. Joint ventures with American companies became healthy. Small businesses actually profited.

In rural areas, farmers not only raised more crops, they also profited from their sales. For the days of dependence on "foreign aid" were over. The massive shipments of surplus grain that the United States had supplied were no longer needed or wanted. Though they had filled a critical need, they had also inhibited national efforts and had forced local food producers into lethargy and bankruptcy.

In the last three decades India has become self-sufficient—not at the level of the West but strongly beyond anything in her previous history. During the period her population was doubling (1950–1980), production of food grains nearly trebled. She is now a grain-exporting nation, whose problems in this area relate principally to sales, storage, and shipping.

So while she remains frustrated by political division, torn by communal strife, intimidated by unpredictable neighbors, and beset by unfinished social agendas, India has nevertheless engineered a precipitous rise. Besides her "successes" in agriculture, she has won her spurs in the industrial realm. Now she builds jet engines; has a plutonium plant; designs and makes computers; has developed a new rocket fuel; and manufactures oil rigs, electronic equipment, and TV receivers. For the most part, she has overcome the problems that plagued her training-cum-production institutes. Now her "scientific research centers" are producing everything from silicon microchips to new varieties of seeds.

To say that she is problem free is fatuous. Though the possibility seems increasingly remote, India could still explode or collapse. For she has still not discovered how to transmit her top-echelon benefits to the man in the rice paddy. Her urban, Westernized elite still gaze—with indifference or perplexity—across the vast economic gulf that separates them from the rural masses. When ponderous bureaucracy is infused with impervious caste, it hopelessly impairs the "trickle down" process. But at the grass roots today vibrant centers have been planted by agencies—indigenous and expatriate—where progress proceeds from the bottom up rather than from the top down.

One day, given the support and encouragement needed, "top down" and "bottom up" will coalesce. By 2100, India is scheduled to be the most populous country in the world. It would be audacious to paint her future in roseate colors. But it is equally irrational to paint that future in the unrelieved black of a few decades ago.

Meanwhile my hand no longer guides the tiller of the little agency that dared to challenge massive odds. But younger, wiser hands extend its impact. Among them, for instance, is area representative Tom Arens, who came to us after seven years service (as volunteer and in-country staff) with the Peace Corps in India.

Finding deputies, led by N. B. Hiremath, through whom he could assist the projects in India, Tom asked for and received permission to establish his headquarters in Nepal. Here was a nation of 13 million people, just coming out of self-chosen isolation and forced to subsist on a per capita income of around seventy dollars a year. Young, well-educated King Birendra had just come to the throne, with aspirations to lift the basic living standards of his people. Tom saw this as an open door for World Neighbors.

One of his first contacts was with the Family Planning Association of Nepal, now aware that their goal required far more than the distribution of contraceptives. World Neighbors was asked to assist in the provision of health and agricultural services.

Through this door has come a series of relationships including groups ranging from the prestigious Social Services National Coordination Council and its members such as the Non-Formal Education Service Centre that works with the Chepangs, a primitive community of "hunters and gatherers." To reach the widely scattered villages involved in these programs requires incredible treks on mountain roads that become trails and down trails that become paths (except in the monsoon season, when they become rivers).

A network of programs has developed, eliciting the attention of development agencies worldwide. Hundreds of thousands of trees, including ipil-ipil (leucaena) trees have been planted—to check erosion, provide fodder, furnish fuel, and enrich the soil (its roots have a nitrogen-setting quality).[6] Better livestock, improved vegetables, nutritious fruits and nuts have been introduced.

The lot of women—once poverty stricken and inferior—has improved. New skills have been taught, old skills improved; markets developed; self-confidence generated.

One of the greatest needs was to relieve the women of a time-consuming drudgery: the securing of needed water for laundry, bathing, cooking, and drinking. Such a task usually involved long trips, often on steep trails, carrying the heavy burden from mountain source to village home.

Even so, only 24 percent of the population had access to potable water. Diarrhea was the biggest killer of Nepal's children—and the main culprit was contaminated water. By the late 1980s a major component had become the construction of an increasing number of "protected" water systems: gravity-flow systems designed to store and deliver spring water to a village, insuring abundant water and abounding health.

Out of all this has come an enthusiastic response to family planning. In many remote mountain villages, the percentage of eligible couples now using some method of birth control rivals Third World records anywhere.

This is, in short, a program of Nepalese for Nepalese—guided only where guidance is needed and wanted, assisted only where help is appropriate and desired.

Remembering the South Asia of the fifties, I am filled with cautious hope. Today, "if we do all we can," we have a *better* than fifty–fifty chance for success.

3

We Reach Out to Africa

By now it had become evident that—at least in parts of Asia—our kind of help had begun to work. But would it work everywhere?

What about places like Africa, with its clash of cultures, tribes, and national ambitions?

I didn't know.

Then came the letter from Ethiopia, written by Alfred Hessler, a county agent whom I had met earlier. Now, in his retirement, he and his wife, Clara, toured the world, keeping a sharp eye out for potential projects. It was a labor of love.

His letter reported that a remarkable couple, Brigadier and Mrs. Dan Sandford, were trying to help some hard-pressed peasants who existed on a per capita income of less than fifty dollars a year. Alfred reported that they needed and would welcome our help.

The brigadier general had helped organize a British military mission that had paved the way for Ethiopia's liberation from the Italians and for the triumphal return of Emperor Haile Selassie to his throne. As a result, Dan had been given a ninety-nine-year lease on a large tract that included bits of the Rift Valley. The farm center was called Mulu.

Dan's wife, Christine, was one of those remarkable women who could write books, take apart a Ford motor and put it back together again, grow prize-winning roses, set a broken leg, or render a classical piano concert—all with exceptional skill. Together they had become increasingly concerned about the well-being of their Galla neighbors. The Gallas, though one of the largest tribes in the nation, were overshadowed—and neglected—by the dominant Amharas. They needed, felt the Sandfords, an opportunity for sound "development."

As part of the routine review, I arranged to visit Mulu. Arriving in August, I carelessly assumed that the weather—in an African nation whose latitude is the same as South India's—would, if anything, be hot. I accordingly carried only lightweight clothes. But August in Ethiopia is the beginning of the "rainy season," when for days on end, the clouds shut out the sun. Mulu lay at an elevation of around 8,000 feet. Because the rivers were in flood, the only way to reach it at that time of year was by horseback, up miles of rocky "track."

We mounted up.

Soon the cold, driving rain that beat down upon our little caravan had turned my ersatz raincoat into a sieve. There was not a dry stitch on me. Water gushed from my boots. The chill cut bone deep.

Well, I had lived through a jungle war; surely, I could endure this trip. But as the altitude climbed my hopes for survival sank. The Sandfords, at least ten years older than I, rode steadily and stolidly up ahead. I pushed my horse up beside them.

"Mrs. Sandford," I shouted, "aren't we about there?"

Turning in her saddle, she said, "You see that range of mountains ahead?" I nodded. "Well, when we get there, we'll be halfway."

Stunned, I dropped back in line. Nothing I could contrive reduced my misery. I was sure of just one thing. I would be a gelid corpse long before we got there.

Somehow I made it and was revived at Mulu by a hot bath.

Out of this untoward beginning came a remarkable program. It began with the construction of a large school—the first one in an 1,800-square-mile radius. Then came an agricultural "laboratory" —to test seed, inoculate cattle, and develop appropriate technology. Finally, mobile health units were introduced—to serve the "market villages" on a rotating basis.

The project became so successful, and the countryside was so delightful, that I persuaded my wife to accompany me on a subsequent visit. It was the first of only two trips she would make abroad in the more than thirty years of my mission. Our long separations were lacerating, for we were deeply in love, begrudging every minute we had to be apart. Yet Kay felt our movement was somehow a "child" given into our nurture. If it needed my time and attention, she would wait and pray and counsel from afar.

Much as we longed to be together, she would not go with me until and unless she could pay her own way.

I felt particularly happy that she would see Ethiopia—the first still-extant kingdom to be mentioned in the Bible (Genesis 2:13); a mosaic of the fabulous—the Queen of Sheba, Marco Polo, Prester John, Moses' wife; an exotic mixture of the Cushitic, Semitic, and Nilotic; the home of the coffee bush and, if the Greeks were right, of the olive tree and the wheat field; an ancient—and vanishing— museum.

After a night at the aging Ras Hotel, the Sandfords gathered us up for the trip to Mulu—this time in an open Land Rover that was constantly filled with swirling dust from the rough but adequate dirt road.

Though our backgrounds were vastly different, Kay and I discovered a real rapport with the devoutly Anglican Sandfords. Perhaps that was one reason they arranged an audience for us with a distinguished friend.

One warm Saturday afternoon, we found ourselves at the Addis Ababa Turf Club. The shadows lengthened as the multilingual, multiracial crowds milled in and out of the colorful booths staffed and, stocked by the various embassies. It was Red Cross field day, and thousands had gathered for the festival cum fund-raising event.

We had been waiting for quite some time in the large wooden building that dominated the race course. Now, as we entered a room we envied the carefree congregation below. For down the long corridor along which we were proceeding sat his imperial majesty, Emperor Haile Selassie.

This exceptional man—slightly over five feet tall, unprepossessing until you looked into his eyes—was one of history's "greats." He had come to the throne at a time of great instability. Through a combination of statesmanship, ruthlessness, and remarkable insight, he had not only checked the slide toward anarchy but had turned the nation—step by cautious step—toward modernity and progress. Much of what he had accomplished, particularly in the field of education, had been deliberately destroyed by the six-year-long Italian occupation. Following his return, in 1941, he had been painfully rebuilding, always hampered by a lack of trained leadership. Shrewdly, cautiously, he had gathered the reins of power until he was not merely a *negus*, chief, but a negus of neguses.

Under his leadership, it was said, more profound changes had been wrought in Ethiopia than in all the previous millennia of her long history. But some of those changes, especially the widening emphasis on education, bode him ill. For he owned most of the land, administering it like a feudal lord. He made all the significant decisions. And his "young lions," fed by the new democratic ideas, were becoming restless. As emperor he was the child of an age that had passed. Events for which he was not prepared had already begun to overwhelm him.

But just now this remarkable man waited for us at a marble-top, ebony table that had been placed in the corner of a completely unadorned room. It starkly and dramatically contrasted with what we would have found had our meeting taken place at the palace (the site originally chosen but altered because of my travel schedule). There we would have nervously edged past a cheetah or two on our way to the throne. Here the only decorative note was a huge bouquet of gladioli in a large cut-glass vase, placed squarely in the center of the table.

Almost hidden by the flowers, his majesty watched, alert but impassive, as we negotiated the long strip of carpet that ended at his feet. In his late sixties, he had a full head of crisp, black hair just beginning to show a touch of gray at the temples. His neatly cropped beard, his heavy eyebrows, and his flowing black cape suggested Mephistopheles—an impression immediately dispelled by his obvious and kindly directness. The palace secretary stood to his left, dressed in a brown business suit and wearing a colorful boutonniere.

Was I another victim of the trap into which most European visitors were said to fall? Almost to the man they seemed to consider Haile Selassie kind and gentle. But some of his own people, it was reported, found him pitiless and arrogant. He had oppressed the Eritreans, planting the seeds of a long and bloody rebellion. What was the truth?

Surely there were indexes. For instance, following his restoration to the throne, he issued a proclamation concerning the Italians. It could have been vengeful and implacable. Three years earlier Mussolini's troops had all but decimated Addis Ababa. Their commanders had assassinated the head of the Ethiopian Church. They had systematically massacred the potential leadership.

Yet, in a great mercy proclamation, issued May 5, 1941, Haile Selassie exhorted his people: "Let us rejoice . . . in the spirit of Christ. Do not return evil for evil. Do not indulge in atrocities. . . .

Take care not to spoil the good name of Ethiopia by acts which are unworthy of the individual."[1]

When we reached what we considered to be an appropriate terminus, we stopped. Kay curtsied; I bowed. The emperor smiled and extended his hand to me. I grasped it, while Kay simply clutched her gloves. Relaxed and leaning back in a chintz-covered wing chair, the emperor indicated chairs for us on his right. We sat.

Since an emperor must always take the lead, I waited for his majesty to speak. He chose to speak in French.

"Have you been in Ethiopia before?" he asked, spreading his cape over the wide arms of his chair.

I told him of the visit when I had, I thought, been destined to freeze. That brought a small laugh, whereupon I proceeded to describe the nature and purpose of our effort in community development.

The emperor nodded. "I have heard of your work," he said, "not only what you are doing here but what is also being done elsewhere. I must say that it is impressive. But why did you choose to come to Ethiopia?"

I had my answer ready. "Your imperial majesty's interest in the education of your people is well known. So when an opportunity to work directly with the Galla people around Mulu was extended to us by Brigadier and Mrs. Sandford, we were happy to come."

The emperor's face lighted up at the mention of the Sandfords. "They are doing what I would like to see done on a much broader scale. We have so much to do to repair the recent damage. I hope you will enlarge and extend your work."

I assured him we would try. "And I would hope, your majesty, that we may have the full cooperation of the palace in expediting shipments of supplies and equipment."

This is frequently one of the serious problems encountered in efforts to help. In Ethiopia at that time almost nothing started or stopped without the emperor's approval.

Apparently not offended by my failure to say *"imperial* majesty,"
Haile Selassie turned in his chair to see that the palace secretary
noted his remarks. "You may be assured," he said, "you will have
our cooperation—especially since it is evident that your reason for
coming is not to enrich yourselves."

I then extended greetings from mutual friends at Oklahoma State
University, which had an impressive project in Ethiopia and expressed my hope that the emperor might once again visit us.

He smiled. "I have a very warm place in my heart for Americans,"
the emperor said, leaning back as though to savor a happy memory.
"And I hope that Americans and Ethiopians can come to know one
another better. But what I would really like," he bent forward with
something that may have been more than a twinkle in his eye, "would
be to come to America again and travel incognito across the country."

There was no missing his message. I wanted to report some of the
progress I felt we were making, but the ledger was still unbalanced
and, besides, racism had been only implied, not actually mentioned.
I smiled ruefully. "It's hard for me to imagine that you could travel
anywhere incognito," I ventured. "But we would be happy to see you
again under any circumstances."

The palace secretary had begun to gather up his papers and was
preparing to rise. Clearly our interview was drawing to a close. So
I wished the emperor every success and thanked him for seeing us.

He nodded. We rose. The audience, scheduled for five minutes,
had lasted fifteen.

We bowed and began an awkward egression from the room—one
does not turn his back on an emperor. After what seemed an
interminable period of backing, I started to look over my shoulder.
How much farther did we have to proceed in reverse? "Don't turn
around!" Kay whispered in a hiss that carried across the room. The
emperor laughed. As we finally reached the door, he called out in
clear and perfect English, "I am happy you came."

Not long thereafter the *Ethiopia Herald,* which mainly chronicled the comings and goings of the royal family, carried this editorial: "The idea of planned community development is a recent one and something quite new to Ethiopia. Yet absence of a programme of community development would have been conspicuous now that we have set out to improve the standard of living of the people with the aid of the development projects inspired by His Imperial Majesty."[2] From that somewhat convoluted statement I gathered that our efforts now had the imprimatur of the emperor himself.

Within eleven years the program at Mulu had become entirely self-sufficient. Schools had multiplied throughout the area. Farmers had prospered. The track over which I'd ridden became a paved road, wide enough for the trucks that served the milk producers' cooperative. We gave it our benediction and transferred our support to other promising projects.

When Dan Sandford, age ninety, died at his home in Mulu, the emperor attended his funeral. Galla leaders, on their horses, rode up to his coffin to lament openly "our father and friend who brought us schools and clinics and roads and work." When Christine wrote Kay and me to report his death, she said, "The seeds you planted are slowly germinating."

But only two years later, in a blood-soaked coup, Major Mengistu Haile Mariam seized power in Ethiopia and began the establishment of a Communist government. Within a year Christine had died and the rest of the Sandford family was forced to flee. In its first year, according to Amnesty International, the regime had killed over ten thousand people and imprisoned a hundred thousand more. Haile Selassie was disposed of, presumably smothered with a pillow. The fate of the rest of the family remains unclear.

If that family perished, they simply shared in the fate of thousands of starving villagers in the countryside. For it had been made clear to Mengistu by his Marxist mentors that his primary task was the consolidation of power. Resources were to go not to stanch suffering and famine but to build up men and munitions. Even when a compassionate West shipped millions of tons of grain to his perishing people, he used that liberality as a tool to force a rural populace into reluctant subservience.

Finally, Abede Kebede, his ambassador to Japan, had enough. Giving up his post, he declared that the Soviet Union and Mengistu's regime had "made the strengthening of the dictatorship of the party its single most important mission, while ignoring the realities that Ethiopia had become a great poor-house, desolate and unfed."[3]

That protest fell on deaf ears. For Mengistu continued to support only collective (state-owned) farms. All help was withheld from the peasant farmer. The result was a reprise in Ethiopia of what Stalin had induced in the Ukraine.

As for our labors among the Ethiopian peasants, we can only hope Christine was right—that, like seeds that retain their vitality after years of entombment, these, too, will germinate when the dark terror has passed and the sun and rain return.

Meanwhile, it had become evident that governments could not only destroy productive programs, they could also destroy people— thousands of them.

Still, in Ethiopia I found the help I so desperately needed. I had come to realize that this immense task upon which I had almost recklessly embarked was too much for me. I had no real knowledge of economics or anthropology and only the most superficial under- standing of agriculture, animal husbandry, and nutrition. Moreover, I had spent ten years traveling among the villages of Asia and Africa, repeatedly falling prey to hepatitis, amebic dysentery, and a host of assorted fevers.

Yet the premise upon which I had ventured was sound. And each new segment of the road provided guideposts to the next.

I discovered that the effective principles were relatively simple. You began, for instance, with the people—just as they were. You listened to and encouraged their hopes and dreams. You invited not only their cooperation but their leadership. You sought for common identity—particularly in those shared spiritual aspirations that would provide a bonding strong enough to override incidental differences. Then together you committed resources—equivalent in their demands—for the accomplishment of an enterprise desired by all participants.

So, somehow, significant projects had been planted or enlarged in strategic sectors of the world. Kay explained that I had a very active guardian angel. She must have been right.

But even with a guardian angel, I could not give projects underway the recurrent attention desired or the specialized counsel they needed. Moreover, I needed more time to study, learn, and share love with my wife and son. Ralph Sanders had come from the Junior Chamber of Commerce to help me splendidly on the domestic side. But overseas I still flew blind.

I needed someone with solid experience and unvarnished dedication. I found him in Addis Ababa. His name was Merlin Bishop; he was one of the most remarkable men I have ever known. He had gone to China in 1935 for the Christian Herald Industrial Mission. His task was to build vocational training schools for Chinese orphans. So well did Merlin succeed that, in 1940, he was co-opted by Fukien Christian University to head up their program of industrial and technical education. When the Japanese invaded in April, 1941, and students and faculty were forced to flee, Merlin stayed behind to preserve what he could of the campus property.

After nearly facing death before a firing squad, he escaped from China in September, 1941. But in 1942, with World War II raging, Merlin and his new bride, Eunice, returned to Asia. They crossed China by truck and train to join Fukien University "in exile." Merlin—competent and incorruptible—was asked to be the director of the United Clearing Board, a banking facility that acted for the many American agencies still involved in China. He also joined the

International YMCA and helped plan their postwar industrial training program, writing textbooks and visiting facilities throughout
China.

On December 7, 1948, the Bishops were forced out of China by
the Communist takeover. After further graduate study in the United
States, in response to an invitation by Haile Selassie, they came to
Ethiopia.

By 1955 Merlin and his Ethiopian staff had completed the YMCA
building in Addis Ababa—the first such structure in the entire
kingdom to be erected by private, local contributions. In his spare
time he also helped establish the first Rotary Club in Ethiopia.

In 1959 I met him, and in 1961 Merlin Bishop became the
overseas director of all our projects. From that point on, he and the
able area representatives we gathered around him provided the
on-site guidance and encouragement to the grass-roots self-help
projects that live and grow in more than twenty of the "developing
areas" of Asia, Africa, and Latin America.

Before Merlin joined us, as the Mau Mau rebellion flickered to its
close, I had made a swift trip to Kenya. *Maybe*, I thought, *after the
bloody forays and savage reprisals, there is a place for a new kind of
love.*

I arrived in Nairobi on Friday, the eve of a bank holiday. At the
American Embassy I was told that absolutely no one would be back
in town until Tuesday. Since I only had limited time there, I
wondered if I had made a big mistake in coming. Who would guide
me? Who would make the necessary contacts?

I soon found out. Over at the colonial offices, into which I
stumbled just as the morning ended, several officials were hard at
work. Among them was Lieutenant Commander J. P. B. Miller—
slight of build, medium height, middle-aged, direct, and impressive. He was the holder, one of his associates later told me, of the
George Cross—an award for exceptional bravery given him during

World War II. Holiday or not, he was hard at work in the Ministry of Community Development.

The clock was just beginning to strike twelve as I walked into his office, and it took no paranormal perception to realize that he was not overjoyed to see me. Nevertheless, he graciously listened to my query as to whether or not there was a need and place in Kenya for a program such as ours.

As I hurried through my presentation, his interest noticeably quickened. He rose from his chair, strode back and forth in front of his desk, and began puffing rapidly on his stubby pipe.

"Have you got a moment?" he asked. "I'd like to give you a bit of background for my answer."

"I have as much time as you're willing to take," I said, pushing deeper into my chair and thanking God for having, at last, found someone willing to listen to a wandering pilgrim.

He walked over to a map and pulled it all the way down.

"First of all, then, this country is literally a preview of hell. We've got three main tribal groups. In eastern Kenya," he said, pointing to the map, "there are the people of the Machakos District, whose land is literally gone, eroded, kaput. We've managed to absorb most of them in the railways, police, and colonial forces. Right now the government is spending immense sums in what I consider to be a totally uneconomic effort to restore the topsoil."

He pointed to another section of the map. "Over on the eastern shore of Lake Victoria are the tribes of the Nyanza District. Their situation is almost at the explosion point. They can't live on the resources now available to them. Meanwhile we're keeping more and more of them alive with our health programs. Soon, I don't know when, they'll boil over."

He paused to knock the dottle from this pipe, then swept his hand up the center of the map. "And here, of course, stretching up to Mount Kenya on both sides, are the Kikuyu. They've already boiled over—you know the Mau Mau story. We're trying to make it possible for them to live. It isn't easy. You may know the land problem. It's held in common by the tribes, and some of the old boys meet and allocate it to individual families. Then the land is divided among the sons and their sons until it's terribly fragmented."

He walked back over to his desk and sat down. I kept looking at the map, trying to visualize the people and the conditions about which he had been talking.

He began again. "One man, you know, may own as much as four acres, almost never more. But it will be divided into five or six patches—a little piece here by a spring, a patch of grazing land, another patch on a hillside—small, uneconomic patches, many of them no larger than the floor of this room. We took advantage of the emergency to force a reallocation. If a man had four acres in six different places, we picked out four acres all together and said, 'Here, this is yours.' But it wasn't always good land, and he wasn't always happy."

He picked up his pipe, filled it again and, after a bit, got it going.

"Frankly, I don't know whether we're doing right or not. Some who are out here don't care. Others do care, but they don't know what to do."

He looked at me to see how much of all this I was assimilating. I tried to look as knowledgeable and appreciative as I could.

He continued, "You know, of course, that this country is made up of six million Africans and three hundred thousand non-Africans. Of that latter figure, about three-fourths are Indian. The Indians don't own land. They live in the cities. Actually, with some exceptions, they live in ghettos; the Africans live in 'preserves,' and the Europeans—about sixty thousand of us—live where we please.

"Believe it or not," he went on, "many of us came out here to help. We wanted to help ourselves and help the African, too. Not everybody felt this way, of course. Some are here simply to fill in the time until they can retire and go home. Others are here to make as much money as they can before this place goes bust. But actually I believe most of us have really tried to help—to help the Africans even as we helped ourselves.

"The only trouble is that the help we've given hasn't been even-handed. That difference is going to get us thrown out. For the African has decided that we must go. He's not concerned right now with improving his country; he's just concerned with getting us out of his land and off his neck."

He paused, and I interrupted, "But I'd like to be hopeful. Isn't it possible that, when the European is 'off his neck,' a once colonial people *will* become concerned with real improvement—and perhaps come up with some sound answers? This seems to have been the pattern in India, at least."

He was a bit impatient. "Yes, I know that's so," he said, with a fling of his hand, "but there is so much to be done. I'm trying to be hopeful, too. I suppose I'm crazy, but in spite of the difficulties and the almost certain disasters ahead, I'm working as though there were some hope of bringing this thing off.

"Some good things *are* happening," he said, a note of cheerfulness in his voice. "We've got over a hundred youth clubs going. You see, there's no schooling possible for most of these youngsters after the fourth grade. So we have all these boys to work on. Most of them are orphans. So many parents, you see, were killed in the emergency. The youth clubs are doing some tremendous things. We're also having considerable success with our women's clubs."

"Why women's clubs?" I protested. "From what I could learn in India, these clubs have been one of the most unproductive aspects of their community-development program."

"Because the men won't work!" he thundered. "They have a tradition of being hunters and warriors, not workers. It's the women who work the ground and carry the wood and bring water on their backs for miles—and have the babies. So we're building, if we can, on the women. In spite of all their work, they still find time—after all, they can't spend the whole year cultivating one acre—to get together for these clubs and classes. They're the hope of Africa.

"And I've been so fascinated," he said, "by what you've told me about your ideas and efforts. They are exactly what has to be done. Whether it can be done here, I don't know. Somehow, it's not the thing that government—or even most people—can see. Government, for instance, will spend literally millions of pounds shooting people after the thing has boiled over. Or they'll invest more millions in some huge economic scheme. But ask for a few thousand for a program to help people help themselves and all you get is talk about how 'we've given you absolutely all that can possibly be found for you!' "

I nodded. I could thoroughly understand.

His voice lowered. He looked down the empty, echoing halls. "If you can come in here and help us, God knows we'll be so glad to have you. If you're as mad as we are, we need and want you—desperately."

I felt a twinge of conscience. He didn't realize how limited our resources were.

"Actually, you see, this government doesn't really believe in 'community development.' "

My eyebrows went up.

"You're thinking, of course, *Then why a* Ministry *of Community Development?*"

I grinned and nodded.

"It's window dressing. It's Gilbert and Sullivan. Those of us who have gone into it are simply licensed lunatics. They give us plenty of paper—we can write voluminous reports—but no money. That way they don't have to worry about our doing anything wrong. We can't *do* anything!

"Well, there you have it. I hope I haven't discouraged you."

He hadn't.

I looked at my watch. It was two o'clock—on a bank holiday! I thanked him as deeply as I dared, and we parted.

The next day, with a tall Kikuyu driver, who introduced himself with the words, "Just call me Slim," I prepared to leave troubled Nairobi. As I walked toward the Land Rover I had rented, a Mau Mau "sweep" was just starting for the Aberdares. For in those dark forests around Mount Kenya, desperate bands of Mau Mau still maintained a foothold, waiting for the time when their god, Ngai, would rain fire upon the British and on the Kikuyus who remained loyal to them. The Mau Mau still darted out of hiding from time to time to terrorize the nearby countryside.

I did not realize my proposed visit to the Kikuyu reserve would take me perilously close to these maddened zealots.

The trip north, with Slim at the wheel, was a voyager's dream. To both sides, a sea of yellow grass, stroked by the steady breeze, flowed smoothly to the far horizon. As we passed Thika, the Fort Hill road, and the Tana River, the rolling hills began their slow and steady surge toward the mountains. Finally we glimpsed the tree-girt shoulders of Mount Kenya, its snowy crest still hidden in the clouds.

Thus we came to Nyeri, to register and receive clearance for travel in the Kikuyu reserve. There, except for an occasional bicycle, I saw nothing that moved on wheels. Everything that had to be transported was carried on the straining backs of women, who, leaning forward, held their sometimes monstrous loads in place by means of a thick headstrap. Across their foreheads these straps had worn deep grooves. But they plodded on, shaven heads bent, uncomplaining.

In the dark brown fields, I saw the women again—babies lashed to their backs—weeding and planting and cultivating. Their only tool was a panga—the large knife that in other parts of the world is called a machete or bolo.

Amid it all, I had conferences: with young colonial camp supervisors, with younger still ex-Mau Mau, with ordinary people in the marketplace. This furious data-gathering expedition left me more confused than instructed. It would take several years before we could make significant commitments.

In the meantime, I returned to Nairobi. Before I left I wanted an authoritative African opinion on the need for and value of such an effort as ours. As I asked around, one name kept surfacing—Tom Mboya, a young labor leader just coming into prominence. He was, I heard, both articulate and influential.

"You will find him over on Victoria Street," I was told, "just back of the yellow bank, over the bicycle shop."

I walked over, found the building, and climbed the wooden stairs to his office.

"I'm sorry," said a kindly clerk, "but the legislative council is meeting, and he is with them."

When I sent a note into the council meeting, Tom Mboya was good enough to come out. He looked me over, his handsome, moon-shaped face impassive.

Mboya was a member of the second largest tribe in Kenya—the Luo, who are Nilotic. But he was highly regarded by the leaders of the largest tribe of all—the Kikuyu, who are Bantu. He had traveled extensively and was regarded as a "coming young man." Generally, he had a Western orientation. He quietly listened as I spoke of my purpose in being there.

"This is all new to me," he answered slowly. "I wonder if your people would be interested in helping us build an integrated secondary school here in Nairobi? There isn't any such school in Kenya at this time."

I promised him that—though we were primarily a village-level, self-help kind of operation—we would give the matter serious attention.

"But let me have more specific details," I urged, "the size, cost, location, likelihood of public acceptance, and so on."

He said that he would but that he had to get back to the council meeting.

That was my last glimpse of Tom Mboya. I never heard from him. But his star continued to rise. When Kenya became independent,

Mboya was named economics minister, and it was said that he was in line to be Jomo Kenyatta's successor. Before that could happen, he was assassinated outside a Nairobi pharmacy by a Kikuyu who had, interestingly enough, been educated in Bulgaria.

I attended a meeting of the Kenya Christian Council. There were fourteen of us present; seven Africans, three Americans, and four British-born Kenyan residents. After a period of pleasant socializing, I raised the question put to me by Tom Mboya: "Is such a school possible and practical here in Nairobi?"

The clatter of teacups gradually died. Several spoke up. Most of the answers were in the affirmative. But some had serious reservations. One of them, a distinguished older African, carefully adjusted his jacket and moved forward in his chair. "The only way I could approve of such a school," he said in slow, measured syllables, "would be if I had the prior assurance that my children would be given a *primary* school training in their own language so that their tribal culture would not be swallowed up by the culture of the larger tribes. Perhaps, after that, an integrated school would be acceptable."

Two of his older associates solemnly nodded their endorsement. I listened in amazement. I had always thought of "integration" as somehow a problem of black and white. But here we were talking about cultures, not colors.

That's actually the problem, isn't it? I said to myself in dawning recognition. *Whether it's Kenya or Kansas, Mombasa or Mobile, tribal culture—and the fear of its dilution—is still more compelling than logic, religion, or anything else.*

But one of the younger men, who had spent two years in America, spoke up impatiently. "It's high time we forgot about tribal languages and customs. Let's remember that the graduates of our schools are going to have to compete with the graduates of the finest Western schools in the world. In this kind of a world, tribes and tribal customs are obsolete!"

His point, I thought, was well taken. But because he was young and his words were brash, his proposal met cold rejection. Few, if any, were ready to forget tribes and tribal customs.

Later, as the Bishops began their constant itineration, projects in Africa multiplied.

One of them was around Mount Elgon. Commander Miller had included this area in his "preview of hell," but the Bishops discovered it to be the center of one of the largest Quaker groups in all the world—the East Africa Yearly Meeting of Friends.

So with the enthusiastic cooperation of this remarkable company, a highly successful food-production program was soon underway. Its theme was "double your maize." Within three years, the Friends Church in this particular area reported an increase in church gifts of $2,520. If this represents a tithe, people of the Abluyah tribe added $25,200 to their income that year—a truly magnificent sum in hard-pressed rural Kenya.

The women, of course, were vitally involved through improved nutrition, maternity health, and family planning. They accomplished miracles.

From Kaimosi other projects sprang up. One of them was with some members of the Maragoli, Nandi, Bukusu, Tiriki, and Ikema tribes, who had settled in a semiwild sector along the banks of Lake Victoria, in Tanzania. The new settlement had been planted several years before I visited. Primitive though it still remained, I was impressed by its remarkable progress.

I was not alone in noting this. Among those who joined me were the Poroko Masai—a segment of that wide-ranging ethnic group that, with their cattle, follow the grass along a wide band in East Africa. One of their chiefs, noting what was happening, sought out Merlin Bishop. Speaking with dignity and deep feeling, the chief told his story.

"My people," he said, "know nothing but cattle. We have always been herdsmen, driving our cattle from well to water hole—as long as there was water. But several years ago the skies refused to give that water. More than ninety out of every hundred of our cattle have died. We would be dead, too, had it not been for food sent to us from abroad.

"But this cannot last. We are a proud people. Even as we eat the food sent to us, we are dying from the inside. From earliest times, we have lived by tribal customs. We have not sought education. Now many of our children want schooling. In our tribal council we have discussed these things. We know we are here today, but no one knows where we will be at the next great moon."

The group that had accompanied him nodded solemnly.

"Things are different today. Nothing used to frighten us. But now we are afraid that we will be swallowed up by the tribes from the north and from the west. We have no schools and no one to teach us. Our cattle are almost gone, and we do not know how to grow other food. We cannot continue to live on gifts. We want to build permanent shambas and learn how to grow maize. We want water holes that won't dry up. We love our cattle, but maybe we have had too many. Can you help us?"

We could try. In not many months we had found three capable village-level workers. These assisted volunteers led the way into projects of food production, health, and education.

Two years later I again visited the Poroko Masai. As I looked at the evidence of progress—the school, the clinic, the growing grain— I felt immensely pleased. But one thing troubled me. As I had been royally entertained by the senior elders I noticed a group of the senior and junior warriors (the moran) standing silently off to one side. They wore full battle regalia and proudly held their cowhide shields and long, bright spears. They seemed to scorn the entire proceedings.

If these younger people, I thought, *are not really in favor of this effort, then it will die with these old men. Our help will be short-term and, in effect, wasted.*

Asking for an interpreter, I walked over to the area where they were grouped and picked out the one who was plainly the leader. He was tall and intimidating, with his face and upper body smeared with the ocher-colored clay that was mined nearby. His hair was rolled into tight ringlets held in place by mud and animal fat.

"You have seen what is going on here," I began, "now I would like to ask you what you think. Do you approve? Will you take part in it?"

Neither he nor any of his band said anything. He simply stared at me—deeply, searchingly.

I tried again. "As you can see, some of your people are planting maize and other crops. They are building clinics and homes. They are, in fact, becoming farmers—a kind of life the Masai have scorned in the past. Is this really what you want?"

I waited for what seemed long minutes. Finally his answer came, "If my father, when he was my age, had known what I know today, I would not be ashamed—as I now am ashamed."

I was amazed at his words. Of all the people least likely to show shame, it is the Masai. They are proud of their culture—their age groups, which respect and defend one another; their physical bravery, which strikes fear to the hearts of all their enemies; their cattle, to which they feel an almost human kinship. Yet I was listening to the self-abasement of a Masai warrior. In a way it echoed what the chief had said two years earlier.

"I am ashamed," he continued, "because all I know, all I can do, is follow cattle and, if need be, fight. Someday I will have children. I don't want them to be like me. I want them to know how to take their place in the 'New Africa' I keep hearing about.

"If you have come to help us find and take that place, you need not worry. You will have us—all we are, all we can do."

I took his hand. He was, I thought, beautiful. I hated to leave him, but of course I had to. To help him and his companions reach real maturity was not to adopt them; it was to release them. It meant

91

providing incentive, eliciting enthusiasm, evoking confidence—and then getting out of the way.

Besides, there were many other projects in Kenya I needed to see—with the Anglicans in the Nakuru District; the British Methodists in the Meru District and along the Tana River; the YMCA at Lake Navasha; the Kenya Family Planning Association; and the National Freedom From Hunger Committee.

I found that, like the biblical sower, some of the seeds we planted fell on stony ground and died. Some fell on shallow soil and brought forth a sickly crop. But most, thank God, had fallen on good soil and had brought forth thirty, sixty, and a hundredfold.

Even as the visits proceeded, there came another call from the Masai. This time it was from Tanzania, where things had not been going well. Since President Julius Nyerere—whose integrity was unquestioned—had embarked upon a socialist (though non-Communist) course, food production steeply declined.

From his headquarters near a place called Longido, one of the Masai chiefs had sent us a call for help. But before we answered, I decided to do a little investigating on my own.

"Just what are these Tanzanian Masai like?" I asked a man who had worked among them.

"Well," he said, "I spent twenty-eight years trying to get a few changes made. I never could. They like things just the way they have always been. They completely ignore outside suggestions." Others who purported to know drew an equally pessimistic picture.

In Longido itself—in Masai the name means "the place of sharpening stone"—we visited the school. It was under the supervision of the Lutherans, who seemed to be doing an excellent job.

The schoolmaster, a member of the Warusha tribe, talked about some of his problems: "The Masai," he said, "are beginning to send quite a few of their children here. But they don't want us to change the way they dress, look, or smell. What they really object to are the baths we force all the children to take. Believe me, most of them really need those baths! But the Masai simply can't stand it when the children come home to their cow-dung bomas smelling of soap. They think soap smells terrible."

We talked about the possibility of change. He thought it would be a long time coming.

"But if one of the chiefs sponsored it," I ventured, "wouldn't that help speed it along?"

"Yes, it would. And it would be a lot better if the—how you say it?—'witch doctor' could be persuaded. The people think of him as almost a god; they do whatever he says."

Finally, far off the main road, we came to the large and impressive boma of the chief who had invited our visit. The boma, incidentally, was home for both people and cattle. It was surrounded by a high, tightly woven hedge of thornbushes designed to keep out predatory animals. Inside lay four beehive-shaped huts, one slightly larger than the others, made of cow dung and mud smeared on a frame of small branches. The chief's four wives had made them. All four women, with their six children, stood boldly noting our approach with barely concealed amusement. I had been told that syphilis was rampant among the Masai. Apparently I was seeing some of the results, for the oldest wife was blind, and the forehead and face of the next oldest was a mass of open sores. The third wife was shaving the head of one of the children, while the fourth nursed a new baby.

The chief, not deigning to introduce his family, led the way into the largest of the huts. The entryway was a low, curved passage that led into the dark interior. Stooping, groping, we found our way to a raised clay platform that evidently served many purposes. We sat on hides that had been worn glassy smooth by the bodies for which they served as mattress and coverlets. Off to one side stood a small enclosure where, at night, the newborn calves were brought. Fresh urine and feces gave a distinct aroma to the general habitat. I could now understand why the Masai objected when the odor of soap was added to this exotic effluvium.

Suddenly I realized that I, too, was an offender. For the pungent smell of burning rubber had begun to fill the air. I was sitting with my feet in the coals of a small, ever-burning fire—something I had not anticipated, since the temperature outside was well over a hundred. The chief, who had surely noticed, said nothing; I presume he thought this was just another strange American custom. Since this was a sort of "respect each other's customs session," he had remained quiet.

As we began to talk the chief made it clear that, like his Kenyan cousins, his people were in trouble. They had too many cattle and too little grass.

"Well, chief," I responded, "what do you want to do about it?"

"For one thing, we would like to begin raising crops. We are now being taxed more than ever before, and we don't want to give cattle as taxes. So we need something else. The only thing we can think of is crops."

"Why don't you go ahead and raise the crops?"

"Simply because we don't have enough water," he answered. "We used to get added water from the bore-hole pumps. When they broke down, the British would repair them. Now when they break, they stay broken. But if we could build a dam between those two nearby hills, we think we could collect enough water in the rainy season to care for our needs."

"Then why don't you build the dam?" I asked.

"Because there are some problems about it that require an engineer. None of our people can deal with them. Do you think your people could find us an engineer?"

Now, representing a private, voluntary agency has some real advantages. One of them is the luxury of candor. I never, for instance, had to consider what might upset the ambassador—or even the bishop. For love—our ruling motivation—does not require equivocation, however kindly. It can, and sometimes should, be surgically direct. So I said, "Chief, before I came down here, I talked to a number of men about working with your people. They all told me that it just couldn't be done, that you never took advice or counsel, that you were a nomadic people who would be moving on before any project could be completed, that your men would fight or follow cattle but were unwilling to work with their hands. Is this true?"

He leaned back, opened up his army-type overcoat—he was the only one in the tribe who had such an overcoat, and he therefore wore it on all important occasions—wiped the sweat off his body with a huge bandanna, rebuttoned the overcoat, and replied, "Always before, people like you have come and said, 'Do this,' or 'Do that,' and we have turned away. But you are different. You are the first white man to crawl into my house with me and to sit and ask questions as you are now doing.

"Yes, we are nomadic. It's the only kind of life we have ever known, following the cattle from place to place. We must soon be leaving *this* place," he added. "It is filling up with ticks, and we must burn it over and move on. But we know we need to change, and we wonder if you are willing to help us."

Well, that was the beginning. We started with an engineer. Whereupon, that branch of the Masai—aided by the Tanzanian YMCA—started on the road to self-reliance.

Back with them a few years later in their new center at Monduli Juu, I watched as teams of Masai warriors—who had replaced their shields and spears with mattocks and spades—dug the foundation for a huge clinic and dispensary. It was designed to serve between 8,000 and 10,000 Masai, who would be coming in from surrounding areas.

These warriors labored under the direction of our project director, Martin Msseemmaa, who, influenced by the Y, had found a vital faith and received a relevant education. He had recently moved up within the tribal structure from senior warrior to junior elder.

The primary interest of the Masai is still their cattle. But they no longer have to burn down their homesteads because of tick infestation; they have built cattle dips. They grow crops and even own tractors. Now they live in houses with windows and adequate ventilation. They have money in the bank. Perhaps most of all, they have pride.

For years I watched the changing face of East Africa—the diminishing wildlife, the tumescent towns, the clashing cultures and contending tribes. But younger hands than mine now shaped our efforts. There were area representatives David Cowling and Keith Wright from Britain—skilled agriculturalists, masters of community development.

There was also Elkanah Odembo Absolom, a Kenyan with multiple talents and an American education. When he returned home, he became a staff member in a well-known foundation. When UNICEF asked if Keith Wright could be spared to direct its widespread health program in Uganda, World Neighbors was happy to appoint Elkanah to a supervisory post at the national level in Kenya.

Joshua Mukusya was secured as a division director. A member of the Akamba tribe, Joshua's home was in Utooni, a village in the Machakos District—described to me earlier as an area "whose land is literally gone, eroded, kaput." But Joshua was no run-of-the-mill villager. His talents had been noted early, and he had received training in two wonderfully complementary disciplines: theology and agriculture. Invited to participate in development programs both within and outside Africa, Joshua was slated for higher posts and increasing responsibility. Then his father passed away.

"In our tribal tradition," Joshua said, "you cannot live away from your home if your father dies. You must return to take over his responsibilities."

So faithful son that he was, Joshua turned his back on his bright prospects and returned to Utooni. A drought gripped the area (which is not unusual in a country that is 87 percent semiarid). Conferences with the village elders led nowhere.

Then Joshua recalled that, many years ago, some British farmers had built subsurface dams in the dry riverbeds that crossed their lands. These were meant primarily to raise the level of water in their wells.

The British were gone, and because the villagers had never been involved—either in the concept or the benefits—the dams had fallen into disuse and neglect. But Joshua felt sure they held the key to a basic community need. He persuaded the government to help him build one in Utooni.

He used a relatively simple process. First, he dug a considerable excavation in a likely looking dry riverbed. Then forms were erected and concrete poured into their four-foot-wide bases. Stones and barbed wire were added, leaving room for two pipes. One, twenty feet long and perforated, was buried in the sand—a "water collector." The other, long enough to protrude from either side of the dam, was incorporated into the structure and joined to the "water collector." Joshua believed that even "dry" riverbeds frequently carried a certain amount of water. In the rainy season, he speculated, the sand retained by the dam would become a sponge, absorbing and holding a significant amount of moisture.

His experiment proved him right. At first there came a trickle of sand-filtered water. Then the trickle became a steady stream that continued to run even after all the village waterpots were filled. He and all his neighbors thanked God that the major problem of their village was solved.

But many other villages had similar needs. Joshua, attempting to help them, asked the government for additional grants. The agent to which the request came turned it down. Joshua, he surmised, had simply been lucky enough to have struck one of the rare springs in his area. The government could not afford to subsidize a scheme with such uncertain prospects.

Then Joshua met Keith Wright, who recognized in Joshua that quality of creative and compassionate leadership World Neighbors seeks. Joshua could inspire people; he could recognize what they really needed and wanted; he could organize.

Today, under Joshua's guidance, a program of underground dams is spreading throughout an area where drought and famine have been familiar and frequent visitors. The cost accountability—in terms of dollars spent and people served—is almost beyond belief. The typical subsurface dam, for instance, costs World Neighbors around $4,000, mainly for cement and pipe. It costs the villagers long days of unstinting labor. But such a dam will provide water for up to 50,000 people. This means that, for an outlay of cash of about $.25 per person, cool, clean, ever-flowing drinking water can be supplied to villagers who, without such a dam, would be forced to migrate or die.

Where every drop of water is a precious gift of life, every act to save those drops is meritorious. So in the Machakos District and beyond, all schools are scheduled to be "water collecting stations," with 2,000 gallon tanks built for rain catchment. Every house is asked to build smaller tanks and jars for the same purpose. Plans and oversight are our only provision. All else is the people's happy chore.

In addition, the villagers of the hilly district have *dug by hand* over 672 miles of terraces to check erosion, build back topsoil, and retain every bit of the occasional rainfall. Because the villagers have put so much of themselves into these dams, tanks, and terraces, they and their children will see that such life-giving structures are constantly maintained.

Now the program is spilling into Uganda—that lovely land that has been so terribly scarred.

*   *   *

When I first saw Uganda, its beauty, its tranquillity, and its apparent prosperity entranced me. The beauty was real, but the tranquillity was deceptive, for the age-old animosities of the Buganda, Lango, and Kakwa tribes were held in check only by the strong hand of the colonial administrators. Its prosperous facade wore thin as the miles stretched outward from Kampala.

In one of these very poor sectors, we found the man who seemed destined to be the channel for a miracle, and he was very open to new ideas. Dick Lyth had been certain that it was God's will for him to give up his post as the British district commissioner in the Sudan. He had been equally sure he had been called to throw in his lot with the Church Missionary Society in Uganda, which had carved out an area of service for him in the desperately poor Kigezi District. There he had been offered, and had accepted, the challenge of developing a farm school.

He proceeded to do so according to the generally accepted pattern: There was basic instruction leading to a junior secondary certificate, and there was a demonstration farm with improved crops, upgraded cattle, and a "deep litter" program for poultry. It looked good and sounded right.

But two things went wrong. First, "graduates"—even of a junior secondary school—felt themselves to be moving out of the cocoon of commonness. They were now embryonic elites; and in Black Africa, as in so much of the Third World, the elite do not work in the dirt with their hands. Education, of whatever sort, is a road away from, not toward, this menial status. Dick's students anticipated white-collar jobs, presumably with the government.

Second, demonstration farms, attractive as they are and as impressive as they seem (especially to expatriate visitors), do not really alter the practices and habits of the village farmers. Only when the country agent or village-level worker sweats with the farmer on his own land and with his own tools, gradually introducing improved practices, will he effect real changes.

So when Merlin Bishop had an opportunity to sit down with Dick Lyth, they had much to discuss.

Several of the farm school students felt called of God to the ministry. The diocese also maintained a theological school, where men who felt called of God to the ministry were trained and then sent back to their villages—villages that in so many instances were too poor to afford them.

"Why don't we," said Merlin, "take this nucleus of dedicated men and turn *them* into village-level workers, with intensive training in how to help the farmer and his family achieve better living? This, too, is part of the Gospel, and it would be the part that would help the individual, build the community, and make possible a self-supporting church."

Dick jumped at the idea.

It would take several years before the long-established institutional machinery could shift gears. When it did, a program called Christian Rural Service was born, for which we provided a small initial budget. England's Christian Aid agreed to long-term support. The Anglican Church of Uganda adopted it as a diocesan concern.

To find the people he needed, Dick Lyth issued the following bulletin: "Wanted—Men and women who are dedicated to helping their neighbors. Must be willing to work hard with long hours and very low pay. Must have a burning love for people and a deep concern for their human and spiritual needs."

More than 150 young people answered the appeal. Out of these, 16 were selected by the local committee.

The program had an amazing reception. Within a year, the 16 full-time men and women were being assisted by a host of voluntary workers, who gave their time and efforts to carrying on the work in the remote areas. Villages prospered. Churches were strengthened. Within two years a decision was made to form a new diocese.[4] A new diocese, of course, calls for a new bishop.

At this time, the late 1960s, "colonialists" were being ousted from positions of authority and replaced by their indigenous counterparts.

All bishops in Uganda were, by now, African. But the members of the new diocese would consider only one man for their bishop—the Englishman, Dick Lyth. After all, he had directed the program that had so deeply changed their lives and so greatly expanded their borders.

Dick protested that the episcopal office should go to an African; that he was, after all, not the "bishop type"; that he was needed in the new Christian Rural Service program. But clergy and parishioners remained adamant. They would have no one else.

Ten months passed while Dick put out one "fleece" after another to try to determine if what the people insisted on was what God approved. Finally, convinced in spite of himself, he was consecrated Bishop Richard Lyth. The Reverend Eric Ruzundana was named as administrator of the CRS.

But the new bishop, despite his changing and increasing responsibilities, kept a paternal eye on the expanding self-help program. From eleven other districts—of Uganda, Kenya, Rwanda, and Burundi—came delegations to observe and adopt its methods.

To guide this expansion, a new provincial program of the CRS was established. Buck Baillie, a former agricultural officer in Kenya, was prevailed upon to direct its fortunes. His territory was huge, involving thousands of miles and requiring almost constant travel. But despite the rigors and dangers and misunderstandings, the program of Christian Rural Service was established as an integral part of many dioceses throughout East Africa.

Commitment and dedication, however, do not guarantee manifest success. Perhaps no two men were more possessed of these qualities than Dick Lyth and Buck Baillie, but both witnessed reversals so severe that they seemed to demolish all the two men had erected.

The problems began with independence. Sir Edward Frederick Mutesa, Kabaka of the Bugandas, was named president of the new republic. But the real power resided in the hands of Prime Minister Milton Obote, a member of the Lango tribe.

As the prime minister's impositions became increasingly heavy, the Buganda revolted. Obote moved against them, and "King Freddie" fled to England, where he died a few years later. Obote thereupon consolidated his power and took for himself the title of president.

Later, believing he had established himself securely enough, Obote decided to travel, leaving matters of state in the hands of Major General Idi Amin—a former sergeant under the British in the King's African Rifles. This turned out to be a strategic error. For Idi Amin, member of the Kakwa tribe, charged Obote with corruption and took over the government. Obote fled to Tanzania.

At first conciliatory, Idi Amin became increasingly despotic. Non-Ugandans, thousands of them long-time residents, were forced to abandon jobs and property and return to the tribal homes of their fathers. Asians were expelled without recourse. Whites were permitted continuing residence only under major humiliation. Most left, including Dick and Nora Lyth—who found their continuing presence a liability to people they loved.

Years of horror followed—torture, robbery, exploitation, and the slaughter of thousands. During this time the Organization of African Unity, which came into being in 1963 for the purpose of ending colonialism on that continent, met in Kampala and elected this bloody despot as its chairman.[5]

The hostel and training center the Kresge Foundation had provided to Christian Rural Service was appropriated by Amin for his personal use.

After eight years of unbridled brutality, the regime—bankrupt and finally discredited—was overthrown by a combination of Tanzanian and rebel Ugandan forces. Milton Obote, once more at the helm, promised a restoration of peace and justice. That promise was short-lived, for within two years Uganda lapsed once again into anarchy. Across the countryside, soldiers and policemen—unpaid, undisciplined, and drunken, angry and torn by intertribal rivalry—preyed on citizens, motorists, or anyone who possessed movable property. Embassies ordered dependents home. International aid agencies packed up and left. Obote's stewardship took on all the stench and semblance of Idi Amin's.

The succeeding regime of Tito Okello left the country in shambles. Uganda faced ever-darkening prospects.

By this time I was beset by serious questions. Could a program of practical love succeed on a continent dominated by tribal, ethnic, economic, religious, and political differences? Would Africa prove that our "sacred mission" was a sentimental fantasy? It looked that way.

Not only had we suffered these reverses in Uganda, but our burgeoning project in Rwanda had perished in the genocidal struggle between the Watutsi and the Bahutu. Our highly productive program in Nigeria had been wiped out by the "Biafran War" and its aftermath. What began as a most promising association with the 3-million-member Kimbanguist Church of Zaire had become a casualty of contentious leadership.

It didn't require an unfriendly government to wipe out the results of a worthy effort; human perversity could do it. But I was closing the books too soon. For the picture was beginning to change. First, a disciplined force called the National Resistance Army brought a significant part of Uganda under control. With their backing, a new and dedicated head of state was installed: President Yoweri Museveni. Slowly but steadily he restored law and order to a considerable section of the nation.

One of his biggest problems was the provision of health services. Hospitals had been destroyed. Clinics had been vandalized. Doctors and nurses had disappeared. In the villages especially, needs were critical. By the thousands, children needlessly suffered and died.

UNICEF became deeply concerned. What was the best and fastest way to serve the greatest number? It was too costly—in terms of time and money—to rebuild medical schools, train doctors and nurses, establish hospitals, refurbish clinics. But where was there an appropriate and adequate alternative?

They found it in some of our community-based health programs. For six years one of our movement's associates, Keith Wright—in cooperation with the African Medical Research and Educational Foundation—had planted and nourished them in key villages throughout Kenya. These comprehensive training programs were centered in the village and involved all the responsible leadership. The heart of the program was a corps of mature women, usually built around a cadre of midwives.

This was no mere primary-health-care extension program. It involved in-depth training in the disciplines of sanitation, nutrition, water conservation and purification, the recognition of infections and the administration of appropriate inoculations, maternal/child care, and family planning. Its results were so impressive that UNICEF asked Keith, with their support, to attempt a "saturation" of such programs across one-fifth of the entire nation of Uganda. If the effort succeeds, a new pattern of proven health delivery could be available to serve a vast and needy Africa, where the ratio of villagers to doctors is about 43,000 to one.

While Africa is enormous—almost four times the size of the United States—the biggest thing about her is the size and complexity of the problems she faces: spreading desertification, a congeries of nations that are but a colonial-forced union of seething antagonisms, civil and regional wars, an unpracticed and ill-equipped bureaucracy, unfathomed poverty, and unchecked disease.

The problems are greatest in Africa's west. Into that fray, facing gargantuan difficulties, we have thrown a team of "giant killers." Providing leadership and encouragement are Peter Gubbels, our area representative, whose skills were honed with the Canadian

University Service Overseas; Beverley Ott, ex-Peace Corps volunteer and teacher; and Habiba Sabit, whose talents and leadership are awesome. Together they head up an indigenous battalion that dares to challenge the all-but-insuperable problems of such nations as Chad, Mali, Ghana, and Burkina Faso. They have, in fact, been asked to guide the efforts of the United Methodist Committee for Overseas Relief in this particular area.

In some portions of West Africa, a new and exciting program has been added. Its goal is the early and extensive spread of functional literacy—something attempted by many groups but that, for a number of reasons, has rarely succeeded.

Guided by Salim Toure and Peter Gubbels, the new approach starts with "numeracy" before literacy. After all, there are only ten numerals as opposed to twenty-six letters. The course adapts the Laubach methods to the World Neighbors principles: awareness raising of the *need* for literacy, keeping the study practical and functional, and making immediate application to local problems (weighing the harvest, comparing yields, recording simple data, and so on). Once numerals are mastered, students are eager to tackle letters.

If our little team does not succeed (as that term is ordinarily defined), still they will not fail. For they, like all our workers, are loving, concerned teachers. They teach principles that enhance dignity; they teach practices that inspire self-reliance. If they are ousted or even slain, the lessons they gave, the hope they kindled, and the examples they provided remain.

"A teacher," Henry Adams once said, "affects eternity."

4

Return to Southeast Asia

About 8,000 miles east of the dust-filled streets of Timbuktu lie the
troubled, palm-circled islands of the Philippines. During World
War II, my interaction with her people—as part of MacArthur's
"liberation army"— had carved a deathless chapter on the tablets
of my mind. In her barrios and backcountry, my eyes had been
opened to human need; in the mud of one of her rain forests, I had
promised God: "I'm going to *do* something."

So when a spread in the *Saturday Evening Post* brought an
invitation to work with a small college on Mindanao, I was predis-
posed to say yes.

Back in Manila, I tried to remember my Tagalog—was it really,
Magandag umaga, Po?—and make the best arrangements for a
flight to Cotabato. The college had presented us with an intriguing
proposal, a plan to bring the primitive Manobos into full, self-reliant
relationship with their new republic. It appealed to us, and a concise
agreement to help had been finalized, but I wanted to find out why
the reports of progress had been so vague.

106

After a brutal ride to Cotabato on an unpressurized plane called *El Economico,* I discovered the telegram announcing my coming had not been received. But a representative of the college was there to meet another visitor who never arrived! Somehow it all worked out.

The college, I learned, ministered to the Manobos, but primarily and typically in a paternalistic fashion. Nothing led me to believe it had prepared these gentle, primitive people for self-reliance, much less leadership. Our agreed priorities had been either misunderstood or ignored. Since no change of policy was in prospect, I had no alternative but to terminate our relationship.

Returning to Manila with a heavy heart, I wanted a day or so to do nothing but rest. But it was not to be. A sharp-eyed newsman had interviewed me on my initial arrival and had chronicled the nature of my interest and concern. A young social worker had seen his report and awaited me when I checked in at my hotel.

He was Ricardo Labez—thin, animated, and intense—a former newspaper reporter now interested in rural rehabilitation. As we lounged in the comfort of my hotel room, I mentioned I had come to the Philippines to check on a program in Mindanao.

"I've got a special interest in that island," I told him. "It was the scene of some of the roughest combat I experienced during World War II."

"Well, then," said Ric, pacing back and forth, "you should talk with Tomas Cabili. He's the senator from Mindanao and a close friend of President Magsaysay. Would you like to meet him?"

"I certainly would."

Early the next morning came a call. Could I meet Ric and Senator Cabili for lunch at the Manila Hotel? I could.

The Tiger of Mindanao lived up to his name. In the hotel lobby he bared his big teeth and growled a loud and cordial greeting. Then, without breaking stride, he ushered us along to a table in a quiet corner overlooking the green lawn that sloped down to the oil-streaked waters of Manila Bay.

We talked, of course, about the island he represented in the Philippine Senate—its beauty, its ruggedness, its size.

"We really had a rough time getting from Macajalar Bay to Malaybalay airstrip," I told him as we waited on our order. "The Japanese had blown up all the bridges, and we had to climb into and out of every ravine—some of the worse I ever saw."

"The Japanese!" he exploded. "*I'm* the one who did that job. I was in charge of security forces on Mindanao, and blowing up those bridges was the last thing I did before I left the island."

I told him he owed me something for the skin and sweat and time his decision had cost me and my fellows. "I'll take this lunch as a down payment."

He responded with a half snort, half grunt.

The meal was good. The conversation—filled with reminiscences—was solid. Then, out of the blue, the senator asked, "By the way, would you like to meet the president?"

"Why . . . , why . . . , sure!"

He signaled a waiter. "Get me a phone," he barked.

In seconds he had the president on the line. An appointment was set for four o'clock that same afternoon. He started to hang up, but the president wanted to talk.

"No. . . . No, of course not. That would be like having a two-headed baby. . . . Well, let 'em yell. Just say Romulo is chairman and that's that. . . . Sure, that's all you need to do." With that he put down the receiver, and the hovering waiter removed the phone.

President Magsaysay had appointed Carlos Romulo—soldier, statesman, president of the Fourth General Assembly of the United Nations, ambassador of the Philippines to the United States, now president of the University of the Philippines—as chairman of his country's delegation to the Conference of Non-Aligned Nations, scheduled to be meeting soon in Bandung, Indonesia. But a group of opposition politicians, "the Recto gang," protested that Romulo was too pro-American. They demanded that *their* man be appointed as cochairman. The telephone conversation apparently settled the issue.

Lunch over, I scurried to the shops. I needed film—and a clean shirt. I barely got into it before Senator Cabili came for me.

Malacanang Palace was impressive, a fitting capital for the "Pearl of the Eastern Sea."

The president was above medium height, built like a football player, and he entered the anteroom to which we had been led, adjusting the coat of his white, slightly rumpled linen suit. I found him impressive, handsome, and cordial.

After Senator Cabili had made the introductions, the president turned to me with a smile. "Sit down and tell me something about your organization, Doctor."

I tried to keep it brief, but I did sketch our purposes and made clear my genuine interest in the Philippines.

His smile deepened. "I'm more than pleased you're here," he said, "and I'd like to ask a favor of you. There's an area around San Luis, Pampanga, that was for many years the stronghold of the Huks. Luis Taruc, their leader, was born there; many of his relatives still live there. But not long ago, we cleared the area of Huks. You know about this Communist-led force, don't you?"

I nodded. I not only knew about the Huks, I also knew about the way Magsaysay had broken their hold when they had formed a ring of iron around the capital city. As defense minister under President Elpidio Quirino, Magsaysay had worked with American military adviser Colonel Edward Lansdale. Together they had implemented a program that not only attempted to meet the legitimate grievances of the Huks but identified and eliminated their hard-core Communist leadership.

"We've got a program going on there," the president continued, "that aims to solve some of the problems that give the Huks an excuse for action—not enough food, no land of their own, no income, that sort of thing. They call this project 'the president's project,' but I haven't been able to help very much. Why don't you visit this area, take a look at what's going on, and see if it isn't something you might want to get involved in."

I said I'd do that. We shook hands. He left us, telling Senator Cabili to follow up.

Before I visited the project, however, I had an obligation to fulfill. Someone from the Manila town hall, noting the newspaper item on my arrival in the Philippines, had asked me to speak to their forum. It was made up, I was given to understand, of the luminaries of the Philippine media. I couldn't make the date they suggested, however. So they insisted I supplement an address already scheduled for Congressman Adam Clayton Powell. Against my better judgment, I agreed.

The evening arrived. I wore my "barong tagalog" shirt—a sort of chemise made of stiffened piña cloth. It was absolutely beautiful until you sat down, whereupon it instantly wrinkled. The audience—American, British, and Filipino—were in everything from very formal to strictly casual.

Adam Clayton Powell, on his way to the Bandung Conference as a stringer for a black newspaper (since he would not have been permitted to attend as a United States Congressman), delivered a magnificent address on the meaning and application of the Constitution of the United States. In spite of all I had heard about his freewheeling life-style, I was proud of him. He scintillated. He held that audience of skeptical newsmongers in the palm of his hand. My remarks would be, I was certain, received as anticlimactic. Besides, it was 9:45 P.M. before I was introduced. The closing hour was supposed to be 10:00.

I used my precious allotment to stress the vital importance of building cultural, spiritual, and economic bridges between nations and people.

This is not, I told myself, *the kind of thing that self-conscious intellectuals are going to respond to.* But to my surprise the chairman, in his closing remarks, said of the meeting: "This is amazing. Here we have two men. One is a congressman, the other is the head of a self-help agency. Yet I've never heard two better sermons in all my life!"

They all cheered. Neither Powell nor I mentioned the fact that we were both preachers: he a Baptist, I a Methodist.

The "president's project" was in many ways a mirror image of projects we had earlier planted in India. Significant progress had been made. Spirits seemed high, and the barrio people seemed genuinely happy. But the morale of the workers was being sorely tested. Their modest salaries were months in arrears; their parents were demanding that they return home; their future was in doubt.

Ricardo Labez, their leader, explained all this to me and to Louis Gehring, an Ohio businessman then assisting me as we brought more overseas projects into being. Ric asked if we could help out. We decided to do so. Programs were extended in Tarlac and initiated on Cebu.

Now, Ric, I knew, had been a newspaper reporter, and reporters, acquainted as they are with so much that is phony and hypocritical, tend to develop—almost for self-protection—a hard crust of cynicism. If this were true in Ric's case, I knew that sooner or later our enterprise would grind to a halt. We had to have the undergirding of a strong spiritual impulse. Only so, could our people sustain the adversities and disappointments they were certain to meet. Only so, could we multiply ourselves in others.

My fears quieted as I listened one day while Ric gave an "orientation lecture" to a group of young volunteers and trainees:

> "You say, 'We are ordinary men and women of small talent
> and limited education. What can *we* do?' Let me tell you that

ordinary men and women—with extraordinary faith, love and dedication—will always accomplish more than those of extraordinary talent and intelligence who lack that faith and love and dedication."

Our little tree had sound roots; it also bore good fruit. For when a mother from one of the villages came to young Ignacio—one of our recent "graduates"—he was ready to respond.

"Can't we," she said tearfully "do something about the poverty and backwardness of our barrio? The only thing our men seem interested in is drinking and gambling. Our women have no pride and receive no respect. The children are growing up to be just like their parents. Isn't there something we can do?"

This was all Ignacio needed to hear. He called a meeting of the community. Local pride was appealed to. Streets were drained. Yards were fenced. Churchyards became attractive nursery schools. Buffalo wallows were transformed into playgrounds. Prizes were awarded. Fiestas were held—enlivened not by local liquor but by progress reports.

Ignacio then suggested they begin the building of a community center—where the barrio could meet as a unit, where classes could be conducted, recreation enjoyed, and activities planned. The barrio was polled to see how many were interested in helping. Almost all were.

"You can have all the bamboo you need," said the principal landowner, "but you'll have to cut and haul it yourselves."

Securing trucks and machetes, the youth clubs brought in the bamboo. Mother's clubs and church groups saved their centavos and pesos for the building. In not too many days, the center was built. Adult literacy classes, sewing classes, games, and crafts became regular barrio activities. The village was on the way to a real transformation.

It was an exercise in community cooperation, the recognition of higher needs, the dedication of persons and resources to a common and worthy goal. It united and elevated all who participated.

As news of this civic regeneration spread, agencies of government became impressed. The new civic center, they decided, had effected the transformation.

This naivete wrought havoc. For in another village our workers had once again preached self-reliance, encouraging the poverty-stricken barrio dwellers to believe they could, on their own initiative, start the climb to dignity and fulfillment. Once again, mothers were saving pesos. Once again, bamboo had been promised. Once again, there was excitement, expectation, and hope. *They* were actually going to do something significant on their own!

Then into the village drove a team of builders. They represented a governmental agency that had been subsidized by an AID grant to build a host of barrio-related "civic centers" throughout the islands. If a civic center could transform *one* village, someone had concluded, a thousand could transform a thousand. They asked for neither advice nor consent. They brought their own materials, their own team, their own concepts. They built a far more elaborate center than the villagers themselves could have constructed.

Construction over, the builders herded all the barrio dwellers they could find before the completed building and took a number of pictures to send to Manila and to Washington, D. C. Then they got in their trucks and drove away.

The villagers, who—except for the pictures—had been completely ignored, now felt completely deflated. The wonderful idea that they could actually do something for themselves had been brutally aborted. The age-old apathy, the conviction of helplessness and worthlessness, returned and prevailed.

Later, when I saw these civic centers on my visits, I would ask, "What are they for?" The villagers replied, "We don't know. We think they're rest houses for traveling politicians." Still later, I saw the buildings, now dilapidated, used by casual buffalo as a retreat from the sun.

When all this was first reported to me, deeply stirred, I made a special call on our embassy in Manila. The ambassador, I felt, would surely understand why this civic-center building program had to be stopped.

But the ambassador was away, and instead I met with a young man who had been at his post only a short time.

When he learned of my recent travels, he asked, "How is it out in the provinces?"

I wondered why he didn't visit them to find out. But he would, of course, have had to depend on some translator. Chances were one in a hundred he would know the local language.

Except for a couple of weekend visits to the delightfully cool resort of Baguio, the only part of the Philippines this "public servant" probably really knew was the little corridor between his air-conditioned apartment and his air-conditioned office.

But I held my tongue and told him the story of the invasion of the civic-center builders, making it clear that I felt they should be stopped at once.

He looked at me in amazement. "Peters," he said, "I don't understand you at all. You've just admitted that you wanted the village people where you're working to have civic centers. You're *getting* civic centers. Now what are you complaining about?"

No explanation I could offer got through to him.

He was typical of so many I met around the world: bright, suave, well educated; thoroughly conversant with geopolitical realities; keenly aware of just how far they could go without offending their host countries and impairing their chances for advancement.[1] They shared cocktails and colloquy with their Western-oriented counterparts, but had little, if any, knowledge of how the grass-roots, rice-paddy *people*—the great, ignored, unwashed majority—actually lived or thought. Consequently the cables that flowed from embassy to State Department were partial and flawed. It was—and is—myopic diplomacy.

We needed, it seemed to me, a new and different kind of attaché—a social-concerns attaché—someone who didn't abhor spending time in a village, who found it congenial to mingle with schoolteachers, priests, farmers, missionaries, and Peace Corps volunteers. Through such a person, we might begin to approach a 20/20 vision of our task.

Meanwhile, despite bureaucratic imbecility, our young trainees had, by 1959, carried the program and spirit of World Neighbors into 126 communities in the islands. Under the loving encouragement of Merlin and Eunice Bishop, those projects spread from Laoag, at the tip of Ilocos Norte, to Zamboanga on the Sulu Sea. As they spread they took on form and substance. Local project directors learned the intricacies of "management by objective." Former illiterates learned to express in writing their long-term and short-term goals—what problems they confronted; how they proposed to deal with those problems; what, specifically, they expected to accomplish in one year, in five years; what the estimated costs would be; and to what degree outside assistance would be matched by local commitment.

Projects differed widely. In Ilocos Norte, I waded and struggled down a major irrigation canal that Marcelino Arucan—a former private pilot—had persuaded the local farmers to build. It was so impressive that *Free World*, the magazine of the United States Information Service, reported, "The World Neighbors initiated installation of an irrigation dam project increased the villagers' annual income by $375,000 (U.S.)." This exceeded, incidentally, our entire investment in the total Philippine program over the first five years of our operation.

This was not the only accomplishment under Arucan's supervision. For our workers in that area had been especially touched by the plight of the "cultural minorities." These groups—the Aetas, Apa-

115

yaos, Balugas, Dumagots, Igorots, and others—occupied pockets of poverty throughout the Philippines. Many Filipinos felt that these peoples were beyond hope of improvement.

"They aren't," they told me, "really able to be helped. They don't want education—and they wouldn't know what to do with it if they had it. Actually, they're just dying off, and it's probably a good thing."

But little by little we discovered that such conventional wisdom was wrong. One of our young men, for instance, learning of the plight of a group in the mountains of central Luzon, made his way to them—by bus, logging truck, and on foot.

At first, they did not know what to make of him. He must, they thought, be a Communist. Who else pushed so far into the back country? Then they speculated he might be a cattle rustler or the missionary of a new religion.

"But I told them," he reported, "that all I had was a heart and hands to help them."

With those tools—plus a big bag of seeds for the starting of vegetable gardens and a knowledge of how self-help is born—he began a process that transformed the area. Where once there was only filth and hopelessness, they established a health center, home toilets, compost pits, literacy classes, and nursery schools.

This project and the work in Zambales brought our program to the attention of Benigno ("Ninoy") Aquino, the "boy mayor" of Concepcion, Tarlac. Whenever possible, he had our workers in his home—for dinner or just for fellowship. They could not know that, years later, he would be murdered as he returned from Marcos-imposed exile in the United States and that his widow would become president of the Republic of the Philippines.

Further north, where eastern Ilocos Norte meets the boundary of the Mountain Province, lay the little settlement of Carasi. Once this was a fertile valley. Then, as mountains were burned and hillsides denuded, the area·became desolate, barren, impoverished. In time, the inhabitants, cut off from outside contacts, became increasingly fearful and suspicious of all strangers. They were, in turn, deemed wild and savage—plagued, it was thought, with headhunting and witchcraft.

But news of their plight reached Marcelino Arucan. He and his workers had completed a year's work with one minority tribe and felt they could cope with conditions in Carasi.

"But why go *there?*" asked one of his knowledgeable friends. "What do you think you can do? The people there are too dumb to be taught new things. Besides, they are withdrawn and superstitious. They'll not accept you, much less understand and appreciate you."

But Celing decided to try.

"I was short on staff members," he said. "Actually there was only one other besides myself in the area at the time. So I decided to challenge one of our lowlander friends who had been training with us for the past year.

"Taking one change of clothing and enough rice to last for a few days, we started out. We took a bus in the direction of Carasi and went as far as the bus would take us. Then we hiked, asking directions from the few passersby we occasionally met.

"I felt that our mission and purpose would be misunderstood if both of us went in together. Also I wanted the privilege of being the first to knock on the door of the hearts of these new friends—an experience I had had only the previous year. But I felt that this privilege belonged to our trainee, Gil Garvida, who would stay among the people of Carasi. So when I felt we were near, I told him, 'From here on you will have to find your own way. Be very careful about yourself, for from here on you represent World Neighbors. This is your test. Your ability to make yourself accepted will measure the worth of your training with us. I'll follow you after two days. So long, and may God be with you.'

"When Gil reached Carasi, they were, as he told me later, indeed suspicious and withdrawn. But somehow he managed to sell himself, and before the day was over, sweating it out with the villagers in their hard farm work, he had been invited to make his home with the local mayor—the chieftain.

"When I arrived two days later, I found myself eagerly welcomed. Garvida had told them that 'a big friend' was arriving. After an early supper, I joined in an assembly of the whole tribe. The chieftain introduced me, telling his people, 'Our prayers have been heard, for He has sent to help us these friends whom we have never met.' His people received his words in serious silence. When I was called on to speak, I found myself so choked up that it took several minutes before I could begin.

"But once started, there seemed to be no end to our conference. We talked throughout the night—the old folks in their G-strings squatting, pipes in their mouths, careful not to disturb the discussions among their leaders; women with sleeping, half-clad children on their laps—sharing our thoughts and our hopes, our laughter and our tears."

When their chieftain-mayor came to Manila to sign the final papers that established full legal claim to their ancestral homesite, he met with a group of our village-level workers. Speaking through an interpreter, he said: "In the first place, my dear friends, I regret to say that I cannot speak to you in your language. But I hope you will understand me, because we are now all brothers.

"I am the mayor of a small community called Carasi, inhabited by a poor, ignorant tribe moving around the mountain. Since 1912 Carasi was with government. But nothing was done to improve the lot of the people; Carasi was known only as a place of the wandering people.

"Some months ago God thought of us in Carasi. He sent the World Neighbors, even though we did not expect them. It was like a miracle that happens to a lost man dying from hunger. They opened our eyes. They gave strength to our faith in ourselves. They brought hope. In my humble case, they gave me an opportunity to come to Manila to discuss our needs with the government. They brought me to new, good friends. I can't tell you how happy I am, but I can tell you that I am even now learning more good things from you.

"I have come here also to invite you all to our first community fiesta. It will not be a fiesta where we can promise you good food and soft beds. But I am happy to tell you that the purpose is more to celebrate our accomplishments. We are in the mountains, but you will not walk, because by ourselves we have opened a road that is five kilometers. Do not be afraid to get sick there, because we have our small barrio community clinic.

"Please do not leave us alone. We will be waiting for you. Thank you."

The story is far from finished.

Just outside Manila lay the sprawling, embittered community of Bago Bantay, comprised of some 950 families, removed seven years earlier, in an urban-renewal program—from their squatter homes within the city boundaries and placed on a barren stretch of land without roads, electric lights, running water, or sanitation. Frustration led to increasing crime. Bago Bantay was an explosive cul-de-sac.

But somebody there had heard about us, and a request for help came in to the training center. Shortly thereafter one of our husband-and-wife teams decided to move to Bago Bantay, to live with the villagers, learn with and from them, and offer them the inspiration needed for a self-help project. Results were dramatic.

The great need was for jobs. So a contract was arranged with the national coconut-fiber industry. Soon 150 workers—men, women, and children, ranging in age from seven to sixty-three—were earning their way by sorting and cleaning and processing this basic and plentiful crop.

Next the community faced its sanitation needs. There were no toilets, no drains, and no garbage collections. Gutters were rivers of sewage, and paths were piled high with trash.

Youth clubs, formed largely for recreation, now undertook the task of garbage disposal. They constructed brick-lined garbage pits. They became enthusiastic builders and salesmen of the World Neighbors sponsored "flush toilet." With a simple mold, a little cement and sand, a passion for environmental sanitation, and a readiness to "do it yourself," they battered down the apathy that met their initial proposals. Now a family could have their own water-sealed and odor-free toilet at a modest price—a third or less of the cost in Manila.

Nutrition classes brought on a campaign for fresh fruits and vegetables. Home-lot gardens became a commonplace. And a truck load of *malungay* seedlings, rich in vitamin A, was secured from the Bureau of Plant Industry. Holes for the seedlings were dug by the barrio people, with tools furnished by CARE.

More wells were dug or deepened. Water from a nearby stream was diverted for irrigation. When an army bulldozer was secured and a farm-to-market road completed to the main highway, the villagers celebrated by lining its borders with whitewashed stones.

As conditions improved in Bago Bantay, some of the women felt that because they had been helped, they must help others—a fundamental tenet of the World Neighbors' message.

A midwife—later trained in mothercraft, health, and sanitation—began the first action. She and several friends had become aware of the pathetic barrio of Bahay Toro, a community of three hundred families just off one of the main roads into Quezon City. They decided to "adopt" it. There they replicated the transformation that had come to them.

This bootstrap accomplishment by the citizens of Bago Bantay did not pass unnoticed. I was greatly moved when the director of the USIA came in person to say:

"Here in Bago Bantay and in the work you, its people, have done to better your lives, is a prime example of what free people everywhere are capable of doing in their own self-interest, and in the interest of their nation and of the free world in general. . . . It is to the lasting credit of World Neighbors and to the communities they work with, that together you have accomplished so much in the face of severe limitations."

Not long thereafter, Roy Ingersoll of Borg-Warner visited the area. Afterwards he said to us:

"As a businessman I have made many investments. And businessmen are interested in results and dividends. I consider my investment in World Neighbors to have been the one that paid the most dividends, gave me the most satisfaction. I had received reports about the program, but now that I have seen the actual results, I can say those reports didn't do the program justice. My heart is full. God bless you all."

Roy could not, of course, see the full sweep of our operation. For by this time more than sixty village-level workers, most of them full-time volunteers with an enabling allowance, labored throughout the provinces. These were, for the most part, unsophisticated, idealistic, dedicated youngsters—going where nobody should be asked to go, doing what nobody should be asked to do. I wondered what made them tick.

So one day in Zambales, I asked one of our hardest workers, "Eddie, why do you work as you do in our program? I happen to know you once served with the Huks. Why did you go with them? And what brought you to us?"

It was not easy for Eddie to tell me. Tears kept filling his eyes. "I was just a kid," he said, his voice breaking now and then, "when they first came to see me. And I didn't know anything about Communism. All I knew was that they were talking to me like a boy courts a girl.

" 'Eddie,' they said, 'we're out to build a better world—a world where your parents won't have to live as they do now, thrown off the land they were cultivating, no job, no home. It will be a world where you and your brothers and sisters can get an education, have jobs, own a piece of ground.' "

He stopped awhile, breathing deeply.

" 'And Eddie,' they said, 'we need you to help us build that kind of world. We can't do it without you. Will you help us?' "

He stopped again. A bus lumbered by. Some chickens cackled in a nearby farmyard.

"So I went with them," he said softly. "I carried a big sending-and-receiving radio on my back. I would climb trees and telephone poles until I couldn't climb anymore. I stayed with them, even when they told me it was a big mistake to believe in God. Because they were trying to build a better world—which was more than most of the people who believed in God were doing. But then they began to stop buses, and machine-gun down the people as they got out—men, women, and children. They said it was necessary; that you can't make an omelet without breaking a few eggs. After a while I couldn't take it any longer. So one night I ran away."

He choked up. I reached over and put my hand on his shoulder.

"But what could I do?" he continued. "I thought I was doing something good—helping to build a better world. Now it seemed to be just a lie.

"It was then," he brightened, "that I met Mr. Labez. He told me about what you were doing. I found that the dream wasn't a lie. There *were* people who were trying to build a better world—only they weren't the Communists!

"I thank God every night," he ended as he turned to go back to his duties, "that He let me find a cause I could really believe in."

Eddie was typical of the scores who had found a cause they could believe in. Most of these were products of the barrio—eager to learn, intent to study, and able to lead. As they were given increasing responsibility they acquired increasing maturity.

Early on, one truth had become glaringly evident to me. Unless the mounting birth rate in the Philippines could be checked, all other efforts at self-help were doomed to eventual failure.

The fact was that the Philippines—though 90 percent Roman Catholic—was readily receptive to family planning. The problem was that the methods most recommended—rhythm, withdrawal, and so on—were least effective. In Quezon City, one of our indigenous staff, Mrs. Belen Garma, decided to attack the problem.

Using graphic audiovisuals—including a quart jar full of tadpoles to illustrate the action of sperm—she began meeting with women's groups throughout the city. Before long, she was invited to address doctors, nurses, midwives, social workers, and clergymen—finally being asked to present her whole program at the East-West Center of the University of Hawaii.

For it had come to be recognized that, without grass-roots "motivators," the doctor-dominated family-planning organizations were monuments to futility.

Belen's passionate eloquence and ingenious presentations won her not only interested hearers but also increasing "acceptors." Orders for various birth-control devices burgeoned. Later, long-term "injectables" such as Depo-Provera would augment these methods. Family planning was becoming a major priority in the Philippine program.

Far to the south, in that sprawling complex called Zamboanga City, I met with Felix and Isabel Rosario. They were in the process of establishing a new center for World Neighbors operations, careful to give attention to what one wise man called "the OBLUTIACS of our people": *O*pinions, *B*eliefs, *L*anguage, *U*sages, *T*raditions, *Id*iosyncracies, *A*rts, *C*ustoms, and *S*uperstitions.

But Isabel had taken up the crusade for family planning. In

churches, clubs, and homes, she preached the virtues of "spacing your children." Many had been waiting for her message.

Sensing a growing interest, Felix set about providing a structure. Already the public-affairs officer for the Regional Council on Foods and Nutrition, he was able to establish seminars in family planning in most of the schools and colleges of western Mindanao.

To augment this, he persuaded three of the major radio stations to schedule family-planning jingles as public-service announcements. They all ended with the plug: "Visit the World Neighbors family-planning clinic." The growing response had forced the establishment of this clinic. Its distinctive feature was that its nurses and doctors had agreed to be available on evenings and Saturdays— hours when most women were able to come, but most governmental clinics were closed. It soon served more patients than any comparable clinic in the Philippines.

Within a year, Felix had received a presidential commendation. Later, he was made president of the Zamboanga City Chapter of the Family Planning Organization of the Philippines and—in a meeting in Makati—was elected to the governing board of the national organization, the first nonmedical person so honored.[2]

As I write, the program has moved toward indigenous autonomy. Different areas now develop their own directions and projects. Some ask for and receive our assistance for new and creative undertakings. Others attract support from kindred agencies. Still others are fully self-reliant. Whatever the situation, they all remain our kinsmen— united in a concern to "build a better world."

Building a better world in the Philippines is no simple assignment. I consider myself fortunate I once knew the man who had seriously embarked on that quest. But none who have followed him were possessed of the integrity and strength that set apart Ramón Magsaysay.

On March 17, 1957, President Magsaysay came down from Manila to Cebu to speak to three schools in the area. Long past midnight, his speaking and visiting over, he came out to the training center we had established there. With him came one of his aides and the son of the beloved elder statesman, ex-president Osmeña. At the Cebu airport more than twenty associates waited impatiently to get back to Manila.

The president asked personal and penetrating questions of our workers, seemed satisfied with the answers he received, sent greetings to his friends in America, and started to leave.

But a timid old man from the village of Nevel got near enough to touch him on the arm. "Sir," he said, "could I ask you something?"

Magsaysay had always tried to find time to listen to even the humblest of his people. He stopped. His tired military aides shook their heads. "Of course," said the president. "What is it?"

"Well, sir," said the villager, twisting his soiled hat in his hands, "I am from a barrio that has never had any water of its own. Our people have carried water for kilometers, in skins and cans and buckets, as long as anyone can remember."

He stopped for a moment. The occasion seemed too much for him. The crowd shuffled restlessly.

"Go ahead," said the president.

"Well, sir," the little man continued, "the World Neighbors worker has told us that if we could get a bit of help and would work very hard, we could pipe water from the big spring at Sitio Potat, which is about twelve kilometers from Nevel."

He paused again.

"And what do you want me to do?" asked Magsaysay.

"If, sir," said the villager, his eyes on the ground, "if you could help us get some pipe, we believe we can find a man who would show us how to connect it and how to bring it across the hills to Nevel."

The president turned to one of his aides. "Stay here," he said, "and see that these people get the pipe they need."

The aide started to protest; Magsaysay raised his hand. The issue was closed. Bidding our workers a final good-bye, the president climbed back into his car and left for the airport. Of his official party, only his unhappy aide remained behind.

In the years to come, this aide was to thank God for the assignment that kept him in Cebu. For less than half an hour later Ramón Magsaysay was dead. His pilot had been unable to clear the towering peaks of nearby Mount Manungal.[3]

Twenty-five of Magsaysay's closest friends perished with him, among them Senator Tomas Cabili. Had the aide not stayed behind to help the villagers of barrio Nevel, he too would undoubtedly have died. For there was only one survivor, a burned and badly injured newspaper reporter. His paper reported that the crash was the consequence of motor failure.

This tragic and untimely disaster was an irreparable loss to the Philippines and the world.

Months later, back again in Cebu, I went up to barrio Nevel to drink some of the first water that came flowing, pure and sweet, across the rocky kilometers. The government had provided the pipe; we had furnished the encouragement and oversight; the people had given their labor.

With the local Catholic priest, I climbed up to Sitio Potat. There, together, we blessed the life-giving spring. It was a ceremony of which President Magsaysay would have approved.

All over the area villagers took me to their hearts. I was made an "adopted son" of the municipality of Barili, an "ambassador" from Guba, a "commissioner of peace" from Lahug.

One barrio where we were just getting acquainted was especially famed for the quality of its mangoes. A farmer brought me some, cradling them carefully in his arms. He smiled proudly.

"Try some of these," he said. "I know you'll like them."

I bit into one. The sweet, tart juice trickled down my chin. It was delicious. I smiled and nodded, my mouth too full for better acknowledgment.

"President Magsaysay liked them, too," said the farmer. "We put four hundred pounds of them in the plane that was to take him back to Manila. Poor fellow, I don't suppose he even got to taste them."

I dropped the last of my mango and could think of nothing to say.

There had, of course, been much speculation that Magsaysay's death was no accident. In support of that theory, Walker Stone, editor-in-chief of the Scripps-Howard Newspapers, reported a conversation he had had with Magsaysay eight days before he was killed. "They're going to try to bump me off," he quoted the president as saying. "They know they can't win if I live." This, Stone felt, was significant.

Sabotage didn't kill Ramón Magsaysay; it was four hundred pounds of misapplied kindness.

When, following Magsaysay's untimely death, Carlos García assumed the presidency, we all speculated whether the reforms that had been set in motion would survive. "Surely," I said to a group of my friends as we rose from a meal of adobo, "his *first* administration will be a good one. After Magsaysay, he'll simply have to establish a reputation for fairness. He'll need to do that to be reelected, won't he?"

One of my grizzled companions looked at me pityingly. "You talk like an American. You've got to start thinking like a Filipino. What García has to do is to accumulate enough money during his *first* administration so that he can *buy* his second one. Why, not many years ago—when I was still an active politico—I used to take two bags of peso notes down to Cebu and buy the votes of the whole island."

His prediction came true. García's term was one of unrelieved corruption; almost everything seemed to be for sale.

During that regime, I once went with a young lawyer out to a troubled barrio. The big landowner, the *haciendero*, had just thrown a group of sharecroppers off the land they were in the process of cultivating. This clearly contravened one of the first laws Magsaysay had pushed through Congress, a tenancy law that assured the sharecropper he would receive 70 percent of his annual crop and would be secure against arbitrary eviction.

But the law was widely ignored. The owner—without providing anything—demanded 50 percent of the crop, and evicted his tenants at whim. This particular group, having been told we were coming, waited for us in front of a sari-sari store.

The young attorney called them together and explained that the law was on *their* side. If they chose to challenge the landlord for his action, he would be glad to represent them in court.

But as he continued to speak, a number of hard-faced men—their sidearms visible and menacing—began to circle our little gathering. The sharecroppers plainly felt uneasy. One by one they slipped away. Then in no uncertain terms, we were told what waited for us if we remained. It was now quite late. Anything could happen.

"Don't worry," said the young lawyer, "we'll go over to my uncle's and spend the night."

But the uncle did not invite us in. "Look," he said, "I've got to live here. And I won't live long if I take in people like you. You'll just have to go somewhere else." With that he shut the door.

We spent the night sleeping as best we could on the floor of an empty house. I thought I was back in the infantry.

"But what about that law?" I asked the next morning as we prepared to return to Manila.

"Well, the truth is," answered the idealistic young attorney, "that the men who put that law on the books are the very men who are determined to see that it is never enforced."

When Diosdado Macapagal—claiming to be, like Magsaysay, a "man of the people"—displaced García, hope was rekindled. He began well, but before he was soundly defeated by Ferdinand

Marcos, in 1965, he had become deeply involved in venality and corruption.

Marcos won the election by promising to clean up the mess. "We have," he declared, "ceased to value order. Justice and security are myths. Our government is gripped in the iron hand of venality, its treasury is barren, its resources are wasted, its civil service is slothful and indifferent, its armed forces demoralized, and its councils sterile."[4]

A highly decorated war hero, he and his beautiful wife Imelda were seen as saviors. They would—they said—check unemployment, restore order, assure justice, provide equity, and eliminate the slums. But in the years that followed, their successive regimes would systematically plunder the nation that had trusted them.

Did their removal by the popular coup of Corazon Aquino— herself a member of the land-owning elite—change the pattern and course of Filipino history? Only time will tell. Mrs. Aquino began by proposing accelerated land reform. But the proposals are hedged about by crippling qualifications, adamantly opposed by the large landholders, and—above all—required to be implemented by the legislature, a body that has consistently demonstrated its intention and ability to scuttle any real land reform.[5]

Belatedly she has tried—à la Ramón Magsaysay—to use the army's Special Operations Teams in social programs designed to win the hearts and loyalties of the depressed and disappointed peasants. Whether these teams can counter the incursions of the Communist-led New People's Army remains to be seen.

In sum, in the Philippines two diverse societies exist. One is more homogeneous than the other, being largely of Spanish derivation and culture. It includes—and, in a sense, is dominated by—the often brilliant, sometimes wealthy, usually ambitious community from whence comes the oligarchy.

But no social group is monolithic. Even within that oligarchy there are fierce divisions, often augmented by regional and/or language differences.

Confronting this ascendant group are the impoverished, disorganized, underemployed or unemployed masses. They are even more divided—tribally, linguistically, and economically. They like the sound of "democracy," though they have seen how fragile and elusive it may be, but they often find themselves more comfortable under the wing of some powerful *patron*. Above all, because they have so little vested interest in their own economy, they are ready targets for subversion by extremists from the left or right.

Poverty is deep and real. The stubborn resistance to significant change by the regnant social group makes a revolutionary scenario increasingly probable. For deferred expectations, entrenched corruption, and pervasive inequity almost inevitably breed terrorism and revolution.

Yet there is hope. Even among the oligarchy many remember the stirring idealism of those revered leaders who led the Philippines out of colonial domination. I also know that in hundreds of barrios up and down the islands, little groups of once discouraged people have tasted self-reliance, found dignity, and extended help. I hope and expect that these potential leaders from all social groups, speaking English, Spanish, or Tagalog, will ultimately unite as champions of stability and peace.

Meanwhile, just over the southwestern horizon, on the far-flung archipelago that stretches more than 3,000 miles along the curve of the Indian Ocean, huge tides of change have rolled ashore.

I first saw Indonesia when, on a trip to India, I stopped off for a brief survey of project opportunities. My host Dr. Alexander Rotti, the national secretary of the YMCA, had spent much of World War II in a Japanese prison camp, where he lost his father, mother, and two sons. Now he tried to fill thirteen different governmental assignments, mainly because he was one of Indonesia's few university-educated Eurasians. I was fortunate, indeed, that he took me under his wing and into his home.

At this time President Achmed Sukarno—whom some said was being "wrapped up like a worm in a cocoon" by the Communists— was in Bandung, welcoming delegates from twenty-nine Afro-Asian nations to a conference called to consider how they might best guide their own destinies. In his opening remarks on April 18, 1955, the president said, "The battle against colonialism has been a long one, and do you know that today is a famous anniversary in that battle? On April 18, 1775, Paul Revere rode at midnight through the New England countryside, warning of the approach of the British troops and the opening of the American War of Independence."

Thus, with a tribute to a Yankee, the Bandung Conference of nonwhite nations, representing more than half the world's people, began its deliberations.

While this was going on, Dr. Rotti was introducing me to Prime Minister Boerhanoedin Harahap. Harahap was a member of the executive committee of the Masjumi Party—the largest of the Muslim political groups.

As I entered his casually furnished office, he rose and greeted me solemnly. For a time we spoke easily of incidentals—mainly about Djakarta's crisis in housing. For the city's population had swelled from .5 million to over 3 million in ten years.

Then the tone changed. "Just why have you come to my country?" the prime minister asked me, brows lowering.

I began to tell him about the program to which I had given my life.

He interrupted, looking sharply at me as he said, "I think I should tell you frankly that we in Indonesia are suspicious of anything from the West. Why have you *actually* come?"

This was not the first time I had met with skepticism. Perhaps I should have expected it even more often.

"Mr. Prime Minister," I replied, "I can understand your suspicion. But the fact is that I represent a group who are not concerned to promote the program of any church or any nation. We are just people—ordinary people—who are trying to meet with and learn from other ordinary people. We believe that, in this way, we may be able to help dispel misunderstanding and to help build world peace. We have no ax to grind, no sectarian purpose to gain; we are simply responding to an impulse and a conviction that we cannot ignore—a man should love his neighbor as himself."

The prime minister watched me with eyes that seemed to probe my very soul.

"By the way," I added, "before I left the Philippines, I secured permission to ask help from any here who might be interested in assisting their Moro brothers in Mindanao. For, as you may have heard, there has been an earthquake in central Mindanao and many mosques have been destroyed. If you, or anyone you know, would like to help, I have here the name of the chairman of the committee to whom you can write."

He took the memorandum I extended, staring at me all the while. The suspicion in his eyes seemed to gradually die.

"Your program is not governmental?" he asked. "Not missionary?"

Once convinced that it was not, he called in others to show me around. Before the day was over, I was in conference with Rajah Nisnoni, who had come to Djakarta from his home in Timor—his first such visit in twenty-six years.

The Rajah, too, wanted to know the purpose of World Neighbors. "Though," he added, "it really isn't necessary to tell me. I belong to a people who can 'smell' your reason for coming as soon as you show up."

Assured that our purpose was right and our program was sound, the Rajah urgently requested that we come to far-off Timor. He made clear, through an interpreter, how badly we were needed. He confirmed what I had previously read: Considerable progress in "community development" had been made in Java and Sumatra, but in Timor, agricultural methods had not changed in centuries.

"We are a cattle-raising country," said Rajah Nisnoni, his big hand lifted as if in supplication, "and we need someone, anyone, who can teach us more about animal husbandry, improved breeding, and meat processing. We also need," he added, "nurses and teachers. How soon can you come?"

He was a big man, the Rajah, and he found it difficult to plead.

We talked about costs—what the Timorese would do, what we would do. And it became apparent that a meaningful program could be started for around $30,000. Considering the significance of the job, this seemed a pittance. Unfortunately we were, at this time, virtual paupers. We had already made commitments that strained our limited resources to the breaking point.

So with real sorrow I had to tell my new friend that all I could do would be to pray, to hope, and to work hard to find the wherewithal to make his dream, and mine, come true. With that we said goodbye.

I flew out of Djakarta really miserable. Though I could not know it, one day we *would* mount health, family planning, water conservation, and food-production programs in Indonesia that would attract international attention. Many would help out, but the major credit belongs to Area Representative Larry Fisher, who, before joining us, had been a visiting instructor in Indonesia.

Under Larry's encouragement—and in cooperation with Catholic and Protestant hospitals, universities, and Indonesian governmental agencies—striking progress in family planning has been made. On North Sulawesi, the rate of natural increase among eligible couples now stands at an impressively low 0.59 percent. On Java, Flores, and Sumba, projects in dry-land farming and water conservation have proved that marginal areas can be made rewardingly productive.

After visiting Larry's work on Sumba, one USAID official described it as "a remarkable success story. Sensitive local and expatriate staff; a steady, modest, open approach; and needed interventions have combined into a potent program at an incredibly low cost in an area with immense problems." Emulation naturally followed.

Even on troubled Timor, Rajah Nisnoni—apparently on his own initiative—put into effect an improved cattle-raising program that has given his district the highest per capita income in the province.

I knew none of this, of course, as I finally found my seat on the plane leaving Djakarta. My seatmate was a businessman. Though born in the British Isles, he had spent most of his adult life outside the United Kingdom. When he learned what I did, he looked pained. "That's typically American, isn't it? It sounds so sentimental."

He went on to tell me that Indonesia had problems no do-gooders could ever solve. "The government is so riddled with corruption it's impossible for a businessman to make a profit. Frankly, I think it's going to take another war to straighten things out."

I glanced over to see if he was serious. He was.

"Well, maybe we are sentimentalists. And there *are* times when solutions look impossible. But when you say, 'Why do you keep doing this? Look how bad things are,' why you sound to me like the misbegotten adviser who would say to a shipwrecked sailor, 'Why do you keep on swimming? Look how far it is to the shore.' "

He picked up a magazine. I tried to sleep.

Back from the service in the Philippines and Korea, Chaplain Peters cannot forget the needs and suffering he observed. *Below:* John and Kay Peters in Oklahoma, during 1951, shortly after the sermon that started World Neighbors.

In India, Dr. Peters *(left)* met with Prime Minister Nehru, who kidded him about the name *neighbors*. The prime minister commented that most of his problems were caused by his neighbors!

In South India, Dr. Peters meets a former Communist who was so impressed by the work at Deenabandupuram, "Home of the Friend of the Poor," that he became a worker in its self-help program.

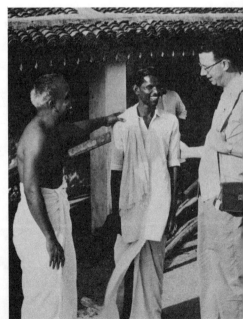

India, 1968, John Peters with
Kerala Gandhi Smarak Nidhi
and a visiting group of geogra-
phers. After he encouraged
them to go to the villages of
India, instead of more temples,
the visitors reported back to
John Peters, "It's the most
exciting thing we've seen in
India." *Right:* Don McNeill, of
the Breakfast Club, was one of
the first to interview John Peters
on nationwide radio.

Tanzania, 1973, World Neighbors introduced the first cream separator to the cattle-raising Masai to encourage sanitation in the handling of milk products and to introduce a commercial note into their economy. *Below:* In Kenya, in 1973, John Peters congratulates the woman who won first prize in all-around farming.

In Ethiopia, John and Kay Peters are greeted by His Imperial Majesty Haile Selassie in the Royal Palace. Their visit came as World Neighbors was beginning self-help programs in Ethiopia with the emperor's blessing.

The local director in Ethiopia outlines the new and spreading problems. Dr. Peters walks with a cane because he had broken a bone in his foot the previous week in South India.

In Zaire, John Peters and Stan Reynolds *(right)* listen as officials of the Kimbanguiste Church tell wonderful stories of accomplishments.

In Ilocos Norte, the Philippines, a previously nomadic group has completed a community center. The sign reads: "Built by the people — inspired by World Neighbors."

John Peters in Galindo, Colombia, in 1965, with some young friends. *Below:* One of the assisted artisans in the back country of Brazil shows John Peters how he makes water filters for the villagers, who drink river water.

In the slums of Salvador, Brazil, John Peters and Father Gardenal discuss the immense problems and the possible solutions. *Below:* Local Presbyterians offer Dr. Peters first-class transportation to the village down-river projects.

5

Splendid Challenge— Splintered Response

As I moved ever westward, looking at projects and possibilities, I was impressed (and depressed) by the fact that mention of the United States often brought forth scorn, suspicion, even hatred. Student groups saw the United States as eager to drop more atomic bombs on Asian babies. College professors saw American capitalism, which had provided such abundance to the common man, as the ultimate evil; it did not pay proper deference to those "natural aristocrats," the intellectuals. Aesthetes sneered at our bourgeois proclivities.

In India a rotund businessman lampooned our foreign policy. With more force than finesse, he really laid it on the line. "Why does the United States," he asked me, "insist on throwing away its money? In your foreign relationships you're always trying to prop up somebody the people are just about ready to unload. Why do you always insist on betting on a dead horse?"

Without waiting for an answer I really didn't have, he plunged ahead: "In fact, you carry on your diplomacy the same way you make

143

love. Now the Frenchman kisses a woman's hand and then notes her reaction before he decides on his next move. The Englishman takes her to dinner and to a show and then says, 'How about coming up to my place for a drink?' But the American pulls out a hundred-dollar bill, slams it on the table and says, 'Okay, baby, what are we waiting for?' "

I promised, if he ever came to America, I'd try to get him an appointment with our State Department.

But once back home in Washington, I sought that appointment for myself. For I was burning to report the deterioration I had observed between the United States and the non-Communist countries of Asia. So not many hours after clearing customs, I sent a memorandum to the State Department. It contained suggestions I hoped would be helpful. If we couldn't change ideologues, perhaps we could counter their spreading influence.

Somehow it found its way to the desk of ex-governor Howard Pyle, an administrative assistant to President Eisenhower. Four days later—surely a postal and bureaucratic miracle!—I received an invitation to come by and see him.

"It's interesting that you should have written such a proposal," said Governor Pyle. He had already eyed me with frank curiosity when, credentials checked and smartly cleared, I at last stood in his office. "Did you know we already had something like this in the works?"

It was my turn to be surprised. "No, I didn't. Can you tell me something about it?"

He could. Theodore Streibert, director of the United States Information Agency, was at that very time in New York exploring the feasibility of a program which had two major emphases. The first was a massive letter-writing campaign. In the recent Italian elections, it seemed, Americans of Italian extraction had been urged to write their relatives back home urging their support for the pro-West candidates. The effort had been so successful that now an enlarged committee was being formed to encourage Americans everywhere— particularly those with friends and family in other lands—to initiate and maintain an active overseas correspondence. It was felt that, in this fashion, much could be done to strengthen pro-American ties.

The second half of the program was to be the responsibility of the armed forces. All men who were scheduled for overseas duty were to be given training designed to make them good "ambassadors."

He stopped. His searching glance bounced across the desk at me. "What do you think of it?"

I was nonplussed. My wartime experience told me the best way for occupation troops to generate goodwill was to *go home*. In their case it was really true that absence made the heart grow fonder. But how to make that clear?

"I think all this is fine as far as it goes," I finally ventured. "But, frankly, it doesn't touch the areas I'm most concerned about—the areas with the greatest need for improved understanding. I'm thinking, for instance, of the rank and file in Asia, Africa, and the Middle East. Most of the people I see in my mind couldn't read a letter if they got one. Even if they could, they could not afford paper or stamps for the maintenance of a merely friendly correspondence. Actually, it isn't correspondence they need or want. What they want is food—and a job."

Governor Pyle, leaning back with his hands on his chest, listened intently. "What about the armed services program?"

"I'm all for it," I replied, deciding that amendment was better than affliction. "But even if it is highly successful, it will still leave most of the developing areas untouched."

The governor lifted an eyebrow. "Then what do you propose?"

I told him about World Neighbors, assuring him we had no corner on our ideas—or on the programs that flowed from them. Any seriously concerned private group could do something similar. I hoped they would.

At that the governor sat sharply forward, pushing some papers impatiently aside. "I think you should go over and see Abbott Washburn," he said with accented earnestness. "He's a man who can really get some wheels turning."

By this time I, too, was on the edge of my chair. "Fine. When do I start?"

He pulled a telephone toward him and dialed. An appointment was arranged.

The session with Abbott Washburn duplicated my conference with Howard Pyle. At the close he asked me to write up my proposals and send him a copy. I said I would, shook hands with him, and left.

Many days later I received a call from Conger Reynolds, chief of the Office of Private Cooperation of the United States Information Agency.

"Can you drop by my office this afternoon or tomorrow?"

I could.

The next morning I learned from Mr. Reynolds that plans were underway for a meeting of private groups and influential individuals from across the country. A people-to-people movement was to be generated that, it was hoped, would bring about improvement in conditions among—and better relations between—the world's estranged citizens. President Eisenhower was scheduled to issue the call.

I left Mr. Reynolds's office in a state of real excitement.

Stopping for lunch at a little restaurant I had recently discovered, I spotted an old acquaintance. He was a hard-bitten, dyspeptic-looking veteran of the Washington scene, and when I had talked to him from time to time, he had made me feel like an airheaded visionary. Now I had something to share with him that would surely make him realize that dreams do have substance—at least sometimes.

He made room for me at his table, and between mouthfuls, I let him in on what was about to happen. He listened with a tired smile.

"Peters," he said when I finally slowed down, "I hate to puncture your balloon, but you've got to understand that nothing happens in this town for the announced reasons. Now this is the way *I* hear it.

"The USIA is in trouble. There's a whole section of the Congress that's very unhappy with the agency. They think it's doing a poor job, and they're about to cut its budget to the bone. The agency has no way to fight back. They don't have the built-in claque that some of the other agencies have. In fact, they're forbidden by Congress from directing any of their output toward the domestic side. This leaves them with nobody they can call on when the going gets rough, nobody they can ask to 'write to your congressman.' So in my opinion, that's the *real* reason for all this eagerness to harness up grass-roots goodwill. They need a down-home base of support."

He read the dismay in my face.

"Well, of course, I could be wrong. And even if I'm right, some good could come out of it after all." With that he pushed back his chair, picked up his check, and left. I sat there for a while.

Man, I thought, *it must be rough to be a cynic. You never can really enjoy an apple because you're sure that somewhere inside there's got to be a worm.*

Anyhow, I couldn't let him bother me. I knew something big was about to happen, and I wanted to be in on it.

The meeting Conger Reynolds had talked about was scheduled for June 12. As the date neared, activity increased: conferences with Theodore Repplier, of the Advertising Council; with Bryce Harlow, of the president's staff; with others. I was asked to prepare an exhibit for the conference on what a "people's organization" could accomplish. I did so.

On June 9 the president underwent an operation for ileitis. The anticipated meeting was indefinitely postponed. My heart sank.

Weeks passed. Then came the impressive brochure—an invitation to attend the "White House Conference on a Program for People-to-People Partnership."

On September 11, 1956, we gathered at the imposing Red Cross Building at Twentieth and E Streets. I was overawed. Directly in front of me was Eddie Rickenbacker, war-hero–president of Eastern Airlines. Two rows down was Frank Stanton of CBS. Just to my right were Senator Knowland of California and George Meany of the AFL-CIO. Across the way was Charles E. Wilson of General Electric. I felt like a Volkswagen amidst a fleet of semitrailers.

After an opening prayer by Edward Elson, Senate chaplain, we were told by Dr. Gabriel Hauge of the president's staff that we had been brought together for the purpose of "devising an infinite variety of communications."

Well, I thought, *at any rate, it's not just a letter-writing campaign. Still, "an infinite variety" is a forest where you can really get lost.*

A few minutes later the president, looking ruddy and healthful, advanced to the center of the platform. Acknowledging the tumultuous applause with smiles, he began to speak. "The purpose of this meeting," he said, grasping the speaker's stand firmly, "is the most worthwhile purpose there is in the world today: to help build the road to peace, to help build the road to an enduring peace."

He went on to declare that while we knew that all people want peace, many portions of the world had come to believe that we actually wanted war. Our task was to find ways of correcting that false impression.

"The problem," he said, turning slowly and seeming to look at each of us, "is for people to get together and to leap governments—if necessary to evade governments—to work out not one method but thousands of methods by which people can gradually learn a little bit more of each other."

My heart sank. I agreed with him completely about "leaping governments." But surely the president would challenge us to a much greater goal than to "learn a little bit more of each other."

"Governments," he went on, warming to his theme, "can do no more than point the way and cooperate and assist in mechanical details. . . . But I am talking about the exchange of professors and students and executives, the providing of technical assistance . . . about doctors helping in the conquering of disease, and of our free labor unions showing other peoples of the world how they work . . . and the real take-home pay that they get."

There it was! More was to come in that same strong vein.

"This way," said the president after a pause in which the only sound was the whirring of an official camera, "I believe, is the truest path to peace. All the other things that we do are mere palliatives. They are holding the line while constructive forces of this kind take effect. Every bomb we can manufacture, every plane, every ship, every gun, in the long run has no purpose other than negative: to give us time to prevent the other fellow from starting a war, since we know we won't.

"The billions we pour into that," he continued with even greater emphasis, "ought to be supported by a great American effort, a positive, constructive effort that leads directly toward what we all want: a true and lasting peace."

With a few parting words, the president waved at his cheering audience and returned, I presumed, to the White House.

My heart was pumping so hard I thought my throat would burst. Could this be the beginning of the fulfillment of that ancient dream, when nations shall "learn war no more"? I ached to have it so.

We sat down. Secretary of State John Foster Dulles, sounding pedantic, reminded us that almost four years ago he had called for greatly increased activity by private agencies in the field of international relations. He told us that we were in the midst of basic and worldwide transformations. Western domination was coming to its close; the new nations henceforth would control their own destiny. The unquestioned industrial domination by the democratic powers was being challenged by an industrialized totalitarianism.

"The problems that arise," said the solemn secretary, "will not be resolved in my time or yours."

He predicted no period of tranquillity—"the world will creak and groan for a long, long time." Adjustments, he said, would be necessary and inescapable. It would be our task to see that those adjustments took place in a context of peace rather than in the midst of devastation. Government, he promised, would do its best to serve those aims and interests.

But a note of real urgency rose in his voice as he declared that governmental policies could succeed only when they were in line with the prevailing current of opinion. The shaping of that current of opinion, he insisted, could be done only by people.

I wanted to have everybody there say, "Amen."

When the secretary of state had been excused to attend a special conference on the Suez crisis, Vice-president Richard Nixon took the floor. He assured us our task was feasible, that in his travels he had found a substantial unity among the widely differing people of the world.

Finally, Sherman Adams—not yet disgraced for the heinous crime of accepting a fur coat—assured us that *this* particular trip to Washington was one of the most necessary any of us had ever made.

Obviously the entire weight of the executive office had been mobilized to underscore the importance and urgency of "a great American effort," a "people's movement." I, for one, needed no convincing.

Then came two days of dogmatic arguments and tentative conclusions. George Meany objected to "cultural exchange" programs with groups behind the Iron Curtain, protesting that they were focused on a government that enthralled its people.

Charles E. Wilson and Charles P. Taft maintained he was wrong.

Frank Stanton, eager to get down to the "nuts and bolts," wanted to know who would pay for the program. Theodore Streibert said we'd be working on that in our committees. We moved into committees, where Stanton's question dominated the agenda. Charles E. Wilson thought he had an answer. The Ford Foundation, he felt, would be glad to help. The American Legion would surely endorse us. Word seeped through that USIA would provide funds for start-up expenses.

Unwisely, as it turned out, I asked permission to speak. "Mr. Chairman," I said, my voice wavering as I fought for self-possession in that impressive crowd. "It happens that I have been involved in a people's effort for several years, and I would like to offer a suggestion."

Permission granted, I cleared my throat and continued, "We have been talking about going to national organizations for endorsement and to foundations for grants and to the public for support. But, as yet, we have reached no conclusion as to what we are actually going to do. Wouldn't it be wise to elect—or select—a board of trustees who could recommend a clear-cut course of action and establish necessary priorities? As things now stand, what could the American Legion endorse, say, except a name? What could a foundation or the American people give to except a good, but still formless idea?"

I shifted awkwardly, not sensing any ground swell of approval. *Cut it short*, urged my better judgment.

"All I mean to say is that I feel the question of raising money waits on the prior question of exactly what that money will be spent for. That, it seems to me, calls for a competent, representative body who can study, evaluate, and determine."

I sat down none too soon, for Eddie Rickenbacker was on his feet. He was almost sputtering.

"I violently object," he snapped. "If we have to go through all of that, I'll be dead before the paperwork is done."

Now, Eddie Rickenbacker was a hero to most of us, including me. He was mightily persuasive. I assumed he was right, but right or wrong, I knew I was licked. Puzzled, I asked him why he so strongly opposed my suggestion. He wasted no time or words.

"Our committee," he said, "the airline executives, is not planning to go to the public for support. We have our own funds."

So over the next few years, the committees went their separate ways. Groups of businessmen, farmers, and stockmen sought out kindred spirits in a series of arranged tours. Teachers, artists, and scientists traded experiences and posts. Chambers of commerce hosted their sister-city counterparts. Bankers feted bankers. Sports associations sponsored visiting teams. Schoolchildren exchanged artwork and letters. It was all good. But it reached so few of the millions about whom I was concerned.

Most of the millions in this country never even heard of People-to-People. On one occasion, I thought I had an opportunity to change all that. For some reason, I had been invited to attend a meeting of the Publishers' Committee. At the long table in a spacious board-room in New York sat editors from *Colliers*, *Look*, *Life*, and other impressive journals of international repute and circulation. Interspersed were two members of community-based groups, plus people from the always-hovering USIA. The question before the house was how could the publishers best respond to the challenge given by President Eisenhower? No one had a ready answer.

Finally, a spokesman from a community group that distributed used books to needy areas overseas proposed that they would be happy to receive and ship abroad any unsold magazines that were returned from the newsstands. It seemed a splendid idea—at first.

One of the editors leaned forward. Stamping out the glowing ash of his cigar, he looked around.

"I anticipated just such a suggestion," he said quietly, "so several weeks ago I got in touch with a number of our foreign distributors. Do you want to know what *they* thought of the idea?"

He waited. No one spoke.

"They said that most of the people who bought their magazines didn't particularly care whether the issue was June or October and that if we were going to start distributing our unsold copies free, we could kiss our overseas markets good-bye."

That settled *that*. There was no debate. The original suggestion was not even voted on.

Then another editor turned to me, "Does your organization have a better idea on how to use unsold magazines?"

His question caught me off guard. I felt as if I *should* have had an answer.

"No," I stumblingly replied, "I don't think we do. But since you asked me, I *do* have a suggestion I would like to offer." They gave me their full attention. "For instance, we're calling all this a 'people-to-people' program. But I haven't seen much done thus far to enlist *people*. It has mostly been a handful of 'leaders' plus our friends from the USIA. Now you gentlemen represent one of the media with the best opportunity to educate the public. Why don't each of you give a full page in your next issue, explaining why this program is so important and inviting every reader to sign the attached coupon and send it in with his pledge of support and cooperation?"

I looked around. Obviously I had once again spoken out of turn.

"Do you realize, Mr. Peters," said one of the spokesmen, who clearly voiced a consensus, "what a full page in one of our magazines would cost?"

Having no idea, I shook my head.

"It would vary, of course. But, at very least, the cost would be thousands of dollars."

I was amazed, not at my reckless temerity but at their contemptible response. After all, I was asking teachers, ex-missionaries, and widows to give generously from their limited funds to help hungry people help themselves and—in view of human need and divine expectation—I thought (and they agreed) that I was doing them a favor. Now the president of the United States had asked top business leaders to "build a lasting peace." Learning that it might actually cost them something, they had miserably recoiled.

The committee meeting adjourned. For days thereafter I was in the doldrums. Then, all unexpectedly, came an invitation from the chairman of a financial association. A luncheon was being scheduled and if I would be in the neighborhood where they were holding their meeting, I was invited to sit at the head table.

This is it! I thought. *Just the opportunity I've been waiting for!* For the plea of Rajah Nisnoni still echoed in my mind. *If publishers can't afford to invest thousands in humanitarian efforts, surely financial leaders can,* I thought. The invitation, I felt, just had to be providential. Hurriedly returning my RSVP, I arranged to be there on the proper date. In fact, I got to the city a day early and secured an appointment with the group's chairman.

Once we were together and he was half reclined behind his gleaming desk, I opened up. "Have you thought about a *project* to lay before the men you're meeting tomorrow?" I asked eagerly.

He rubbed the five-o'clock shadow on his chin. "Well, in a way," he said, "but do *you* have something in mind?"

Without further ado I outlined the situation in Indonesia: the need, the threat, the opportunity, the significant beginning that could be made for so little. I showed him the plan and the budget.

"You wouldn't believe what an impact could be made for just thirty thousand dollars. And it's people to people in the very best sense."

He pursed his lips. "Well, I'll tell you. I think it would be premature to propose anything like that at this luncheon. Frankly, I don't think we're in any position to consider it. But you might leave a copy of this proposal with me. You never know."

After the luncheon I knew.

The men listened attentively to one brisk speech and then, laboring to digest their London broils, went to sleep while a junior deputy from Washington *read* them a cumbrous message laden with the usual bureaucratic jargon.

But the chairman knew what to do. "You all thought," he said as he rapped them awake, "that we were going to ask you for some money. But relax. We're not. People to People is something you can do without writing a check. It's something you can practice on your way to work, or at your club. For instance, when you see someone walking down the street looking rather lost—a foreigner, perhaps— don't just pass him by. Go over. Stick out your hand. Tell him you're glad to see him. Make him feel welcome. That's the way to let such people know that we're their friends. That's the way to build the kind of relationships we've got to have."

He pointed out other costless ways that would build understanding and goodwill. Then he sat down to a hearty round of applause.

Flashbulbs, congratulations, and the luncheon was over. The financial wizards looked confused and relieved. I felt depressed and betrayed. If Rajah Nisnoni ever got any help, it would not be from *this* quarter.

"This may be a 'people's movement,' " I muttered, "but who could call it 'a great American effort'?"

I was not the only one to feel the sting of blighted hopes. There was, for instance, Charles E. Wilson, head of the War Production Board in World War II. Retired, for a time, from General Electric, he had accepted the chairmanship of the People to People Foundation—the "man in charge," though USIA continued to exercise general oversight. He had turned down an exceptionally prosperous business opportunity because the president wanted him for this job. Fired by the importance of the task, he had accepted.

He had shown me an outline of the many programs underway and had spoken with enthusiasm of the challenges which lay ahead. How I admired him. Two years later frustration had replaced his enthusiasm. He seemed perplexed, beaten. Without the backing he expected, he had not been able to put those plans into action.

I knew how he felt.

Part of the problem was that USIA would not be willing—for a long, long time—to permit the baby they had delivered to really stand on its own feet. Correspondingly the baby—as long as it was spoon-fed at the government's table—seemed quite satisfied to crawl.

Some saw the huge challenge and tried to respond accordingly.

Others, like Eddie Rickenbacker, apparently thought a gesture or two was enough. For though he agreed to become a trustee of People to People (finally convinced that having trustees was not such a bad idea), he did not deem that role sufficiently significant to have it—or *anything* about People to People—mentioned in his lengthy biography.

Eisenhower's appeal was not forgotten, of course. President Nixon, at his inaugural in 1968, sounded the call to arms once again. "Our greatest need now," he said, "is to reach beyond government to enlist the legions of the concerned and the committed."[1] His words stirred new hope, but the "enlistment" campaign never made the headlines.

Meanwhile, desperately needed programs of self-help and development remained on hold.

6

Opportunities South of Our Border

Six months before President Eisenhower's White House conference on People to People, I participated in a world affairs week in Dallas, Texas. Governor Harold Stassen was the featured, if not exactly coruscating, speaker at the banquet. Ambassadors from almost every part of the world were present. I was there because of our grass-roots projects in India, Africa, and the Philippines.

Between our assignments of speaking to civic groups, schools, and churches, we had opportunities to engage in some cross-cultural chitchat. At the banquet, for instance, I sat next to an ambassador from a Middle Eastern nation. He asked me what I did, and I told him. His eyes brightened.

"Do you have to be a Christian to be a World Neighbor?" he asked.

"Well, I am—and this program sprang from a Christian imperative, but we welcome *anyone* who cares deeply enough about people to want to help them help themselves."

His fist pounded the table; the silverware bounced and clattered. Startled diners looked up.

"That's great," he exploded. "Why *shouldn't* we work together on such a project. I'm a Semite, you know, and a Muslim. I grew up with two other young men who are also Semitic. One's a Jew and the other is a Christian. We're friends, *real* friends. But we've never worked together on anything. It would be wonderful if we could all be World Neighbors.

"I'll tell you what," he continued, "if you'll come to my country, I'll give you villages to work with and a good man to help you. What do you say?"

This scholarly, modern aristocrat caught me off guard. He had offered substantial resources. How should I respond?

"I have to clear things like that with my board," I answered. Then I expressed firm but cautious interest.

"It's a deal," he answered, telling me to look him up when I visited his country.

We were never able to work out the arrangements.

Another to whom I listened with real interest was Jose Luis Cruz-Salazar, the young and articulate ambassador from Guatemala. In his discussions, he reported that Guatemala had been the first target in a Communist plot to take over our hemisphere. "They work from the top down," he said, "professors, labor leaders, politicians—all seeking to control and engulf the country. They take advantage of the passionate desire in Latin America to develop resources and improve the living standards of the people. But of course they actually seek the power to install dictatorships."

That explained, he told us, why the 1954 overthrow of the Communist-dominated government of President Jacobo Arbenz Guzmán by the Western-oriented government of President Carlos Castillo Armas was such a crucial victory. Castillo Armas, he said, was now helping the people see that their needs and desires could best be attained by a dynamic, democratic society. Toward that end, he was now "launching land reforms, building highways, and starting an intensive educational program."

Up to that point, my knowledge of Latin America was—like that of so many of my contemporaries—completely superficial. Though I had a degree in history, my attention all through school had been directed far more to the dynasties of Europe and Asia than it had to the nations that comprised the southern half of my own hemisphere. These were, I had come to feel, a highly temperamental group, speaking Spanish or Portuguese and enjoying a host of miniwars and pocket revolutions while growing a lot of coffee and bananas.

But the ambassador from Guatemala assured me that, in his country at least, the turbulence was under control and the well-being of the people was being enhanced. I naively felt comforted.

However, Armas's new "program for the people" consisted primarily of quashing the national literacy campaign begun by his predecessor, canceling the voting rights of all illiterates (thus disqualifying 70 percent of the populace), disbanding labor unions, reducing the already low minimum wage, and establishing strict press censorship.

As time passed my gullibility waned, and my curiosity waxed.

So when Merlin Bishop became our vice-president for Overseas Program, I asked him to make an exploratory tour in Latin America. There he met with and asked questions of officials, businessmen, social workers, students, priests, missionaries, and ex-campesinos who had left the countryside and crowded into the *barriadas* (slums). He put his conclusions into a report depicting vast discrepancies, general indifference, pervasive corruption, and unmitigated oppression. We determined to help if we could.

Our first real opportunity arrived on the wings of an invitation from a remarkable man, Dr. Carroll Behrhorst. He had left Winfield, Kansas, where he had been the nineteenth physician in a town of less than 50,000, to go to the Chimaltenango District of Guatemala, where he was one of only two doctors among more than 200,000 Cakchiquel Indians.

These Indians were quiet, hard-working survivors of the tides of conquest that had swept over the Highland Maya. They were suspicious of all "gringos"—as they had every right to be. But within a remarkably short time, Dr. Behrhorst's sensitivity and skill had won their confidence and affection. He opened an office in the central town of Chimaltenango and began to minister to the ills of his neighbors. They kept him busy.

However, as he soon discovered, the most skilled application of curative medicine was not enough. He could get people well, but he couldn't keep them well. Poor nutrition, inadequate sanitation, and unchecked contagion all kept bringing the same patients back to his overcrowded clinic, a couple of rented adobe houses. Like so many mission hospitals, he was "running an ambulance to the foot of the cliff when he should have been building a fence around the edge of that cliff." But he was so busy tending to casualties that he had no time to build the "fence." He sent World Neighbors an SOS.

Fortunately, we had added to our staff the talented and sensitive Oramel Greene. An experienced architect of a successful rural development program in Puerto Rico, fluent in Spanish (and later in Portuguese and Haitian Creole), Orm became the regional director for our Latin American program. He met and counseled with Dr. Behrhorst.

Out of that 1963 consultation came a remarkable project. The clinic and its environs emerged as a training center. To it, from a circle of about fifty villages, came eager young Cakchiquels, chosen by their peers and elders.

When I first walked among these trainees, it quickly became evident that they really were "chosen people" with intense dedication and obvious ability. Some elected the "healing" curriculum, learning how to recognize symptoms, prescribe proper dosages, administer inoculations, and above all, how to institute effective child care. Others chose the "feeding" curriculum: how to test soil, build compost, use fertilizer, check erosion, conserve water, improve animal husbandry, select seeds, and harvest and market crops. Some undertook to do both.

Bus fare and a lunch were provided for the one-day-a-week classes held at the training center. But the biggest investment was the peerless staff: Paul and Mary McKay and Roland Bunch. Both men had degrees in international agriculture. Mary specialized in child care and nutrition. All had previously served with the American Friends.

The project flourished. Infant mortality plunged. Wheat production rose. Corn production increased from an average of fourteen bushels to the acre to better than forty bushels. Some produced as many as sixty; two topped the list with one hundred.

Chickens, pigs, potatoes, and fruit trees added nutrition and profit. Family planning was asked for and received. Roads were improved. New land was purchased and improved. It was the beginning of a new day for the Indians of the Chimaltenango area.

At the end of eight years, it was proposed that a new project site be chosen. The place decided upon was San Martin Jelotipeque, one of the poorest settlements in the area. The training staff would come from the field-tested leaders of the Chimaltenango program, including a contingent of "visiting nurses" who, with courses ranging from kitchen gardens to family planning, transformed the women's attitudes and practices. It was Indian teaching Indian; because it was, results took an almost quantum leap.

By this time, Roland Bunch had developed an effective system of guidelines and technological practices. These varied according to local needs and priorities. But in general they included:

The use of contour irrigation ditches and rock-wall barriers.

Good, deep soil preparation, incorporating all available organic matter—especially the cheap and abundant green manure.

The transplantation of clover for cattle feed.

Control of diseases and insects, as required.

The practices were introduced as a kind of "reverse pyramid." The first year only the most needed practice was introduced and mastered. The second year another was added—and so on until the complete "package" became a natural course of procedure to the campesino.

This system became the key to undreamed-of productivity. Assisted by a grant from Oxfam of England, a cooperative—combining sales and marketing with savings and loan—grew and prospered.

By 1973 the co-op distributed 54,000 one-hundred-pound bags of fertilizer, valued at $238,000, to more than 5,000 small farmers throughout that area. And in 1975 the government of Guatemala granted the cooperative a twenty-five-year low-interest loan of $500,000.

In October, 1976, came the Guatemalan earthquake. Some 22,000 people died. More than 74,000 were injured. A million were left homeless. San Martin was more than 90 percent destroyed. But none of our eighty-four "assisted volunteers" involved in the San Martin project was killed. These workers immediately formed committees to organize aid for the injured and help direct the plethora of relief supplies that came surging into the country.

Some of this well-meant outpouring was, indeed, needed—blankets and milk and certain prepared high-protein foods. But as it continued to pour in it added to the disruption and disaster. Soon piles of free food filled docks and warehouses. The surplus had to go *somewhere*. It flooded into the western highlands. Said the International Disaster Institute: "In Guatemala. . . . 25,400 tons of unneeded food sent by two private agencies. . . . glutted the market and depressed the local price of corn by 40 percent."[1]

The small farmer became the principal victim. The only resources he had with which to reconstruct his life were his own labor and a recently harvested bumper crop—perhaps his best ever. The unrestricted free food, so deeply cheapening the value of his grain, simply wiped out his major asset.

Finally, to stop this increasing calamity to the already battered highlander, in May, 1977, the government of Guatemala decreed that no more basic grains could be imported. The offending relief organizations dodged the decree by shipping flour.

To complicate the scene, a few agencies arrived with orders to construct thousands of "temporary" residences. To meet deadlines, hundreds of villages were bulldozed—burying ever deeper the grain, artifacts, and personal possessions of the campesinos.

Our people had an alternative plan. With Oxfam's help, a specialist in disaster rehabilitation, Frederick Cuny, was brought in. He was convinced of the superior virtues of self-help. Like World Neighbors, he took time for in-depth consultations with indigenous leaders. Following this, about 250 campesinos, in 48 villages, were carefully instructed in how to build (and how to teach others to build) earthquake-resistant houses: erect corner posts and uprights, build lightweight walls, cross-brace the main uprights, and add a lightweight roof.

Commenting on this approach, the *Wall Street Journal* later said:

> The only import was corrugated metal sheets for roofing . . . less likely to cause injury if it falls. . . .
>
> A key element was that "the program did not *give* anybody housing" says Mary McKay. . . . "To make sure that the villagers wanted what they were getting, nothing was donated outright" [though the price of some building supplies was subsidized], and all construction was done by Guatemalans. . . .
>
> The Guatemalan project was one of the first to reflect the growing belief that victims often had enough spunk to take care of themselves. . . . But it caught on quickly. Close to a dozen private agencies and church groups copied it in Guatemala. The U.S. Agency for International Development borrowed part of it, buying hundreds of thousands of the corrugated metal sheets to distribute to Guatemalans at subsidized prices.[2]

For our staff, however, overburdened by this new emergency, there was no time to relax. To the huge disaster they responded with the kind of ability and initiative that, until now, almost no one had been willing to grant to campesinos. It is good that they did. For the United States Agency for International Development had decided to do a worldwide study of "locally based development programs." San Martin was one of forty-one chosen for inspection.

When the study was concluded, Development Alternatives (the agency chosen to do the inspection) reported to USAID that the San Martin program, in spite of its disruption by the earthquake, was many evaluation points above all the others.

The 170-page report summarized its findings:

> The San Martin program has been extremely successful. The goals of increasing corn yields and reversing declining soil fertility have been met many times over. . . . Both individuals and organizations have come to see the tremendous yield increases for themselves. Nearly 700 visitors were received by the cooperative in 1977. . . .
>
> In this program, members are taught the methods and benefits of erosion control and increased soil fertility. They are given no further aid, except for supervision and advice. . . . The project was designed . . . to reduce farmer dependence on outside agencies, and to encourage farmers to be more self-reliant.
>
> In 1978 U.S.A.I.D. . . . proposed that the Chimaltenango area, including San Martin, be involved in a regional soil improvement program. Small farmers would be paid to practice many of the same soil conservation techniques that farmers were already doing on their own as part of the World Neighbors/ Oxfam program. When the leaders of the program learned of this, they circulated a petition demanding to be excluded . . . much to the dismay of AID personnel who could not understand why. . . .

. . . The promotional and technical activities provided are almost self-generating. . . . The viability of the cooperative is impressive. Financially, it is on excellent footing.

. . . The average net income of a farmer, who has been using the improved technological package for five years on one hectare of corn and one of beans, has increased over 1,600 percent.[3]

This was success far beyond our expectations.

The 1979 report concluded with words that carried more portent than we knew: " . . . Primarily due to increases in income, farmers no longer are forced to seek work on the nearby haciendas."[4]

What should have been the onset of independence became instead the beginning of decimation. For in the months that followed, the indigenous leaders of that program—who had brought their fellow campesinos to the point where they were "no longer forced to seek work on the nearby haciendas"—were marked for death and hunted down like animals. We had failed to reckon with the economic and social patterns of the environment in which we operated.

For Guatemala, one of the world's most attractive countries, has an unstable and troubled political history. From its earliest days—as it gained independence from Spain, Mexico, and its partners in the United Provinces of Central America—the nation has been a cockpit of competing ideologies and ambitions. Early on, it proclaimed itself a republic, to be governed by democratic principles. Its constitution was one of the finest.

Yet elections in Guatemala became regularly suspect. A long retinue of would-be presidents—after challenging or dispensing with elections—came to office through military coups. Their terms varied in length, lasting from a few days to a full six years. Not surprisingly, during the regimes of some of these caudillos, the constitution was either capriciously interpreted or completely ignored.

Guatemala's Indians, concentrated in the highlands and numbering more than half the population, were in a nebulous category, valued primarily as a source of cheap labor, especially in the agricultural areas. As one observer reported: "Until the revolution of 1944 each Indian was required to carry an identity card noting the number of days he had worked—for someone else. If he had worked fewer than 150 days, he was arrested and set to work on the roads."[5]

In succeeding decades, caught between the upper and nether millstones of terrorist guerillas and ruthless security forces, thousands of Indians would perish miserably.

The conflict that would consume them began when calls for reform—from idealistic university students and a few young military officers—were ignored. Around 1959, embittered by the United States backed coups that effectively blocked any move toward democracy and inspired by the victory of Fidel Castro's brigade in Cuba, some of these "reformers" took to the hills. At first they were regarded as mere romantics. But gradually they became battle-toughened guerillas, increasingly wedded to a Marxist-Leninist ideology. Numbering at first only a few hundred, they nevertheless wrought havoc as they overran remote army and police posts and then faded back into the shelter of the protective hills. By the time I arrived in Guatemala, they were thoroughly feared. In response to this perceived threat, a counterinsurgency campaign began, which took thousands of lives—mostly innocent campesinos—before it was through.

At first the work at Chimaltenango—and later at San Martin—was never involved in these bloody ordeals. And General Kjell Laugerud Garcia—who almost laughingly admitted that he had stolen his election from General Efrain Rios Montt—seemed genuinely impressed with the remarkable progress made by the campesinos. He even came in person to congratulate them and to join their cooperative. He then selected one of their number to be a special adviser to his commission on rural reform.

The campesino gave some remarkably sound advice. When asked, "What are we doing wrong?" he replied, "You're scratching where we don't itch." It was a memorable line, often repeated.

But the pendulum was beginning to swing, and in the rigged election of 1978, General Romeo Lucas García was installed as president. He began at once to root out almost anything not directly identified with his conservative coalition. His pursuit was wide and indiscriminate.

The first year and a half of his regime has been described in a 133-page report issued by the Organization of American States in October, 1981. It delineates the torture and murder of thousands of campesinos, hundreds of political and labor leaders, and scores of journalists, teachers, lawyers, and judges. Says a portion of the report:

> As a rule, when the bodies were discovered, they appear brutally disfigured, nude and without documents or signs of identification. . . . When dealing with members of Indian or rural communities, whole populations have been decimated; . . . their bodies have been found already decomposed and rotting, buried together in a large common grave. . . . this violence has been either instigated or tolerated by the government, which has not taken steps to contain it.[6]

These conclusions were shared by almost every periodical whose reporters covered the scene.

At this time, when the surging tide of terror and repression was at its height, our project at San Martin was being acclaimed as number one of all "locally based development programs." In the eyes of many it was laudable and remarkable that we had brought poverty-plagued campesinos to the point where they were no longer forced to seek work on the nearby haciendas. But to others, what we had done was an impermissible violation of long-established tradition.

For in Guatemala, as in so much of Latin America, peasants are *supposed* to be at the service of the upper classes. Because they are who they are, they gain virtue only through humility and service. The upper classes, on the other hand, are—on the basis of their status alone—*entitled* to be served. This is a relationship almost as "ordained" as the caste responsibilities of village Hinduism.

So if campesinos generally became "independent," this would call for changes the society was not ready to tolerate. At this time, one of the essentials of the Guatemalan agricultural economy was an abundance of cheap labor. To the owners of haciendas in the Indian Highlands, of whom President Lucas was one of the largest, what we had done was disruptive, even subversive.

There *was* subversion in the department of Chimaltenango. From their hiding places in the nearby mountains, Marxist guerillas made swift, surgical strikes, assassinating selected hacienda owners and government informers. Among their several targets was the police station in San Martin.

In retaliation, government troops, reluctant to plunge into the ravines and forests into which the guerillas had fled, sought for culprits in the villages themselves. Eyewitness accounts have provided graphic details of what went on.

One morning in February, 1980, a village into which self-help programs had been introduced—together with seven other nearby villages—began ringing with machine-gun fire. All four ways of leaving the group of villages were blocked. Members of the Guatemalan army, revenue agents, and undercover security guards manned the blockades.

These groups entered the villages, killing any man who tried to escape. Once there, they systematically sought out and murdered all suspected of having any kind of leadership role. Most of these were garroted with thin, plastic cord; then their bodies were tied to horses and dragged to hinder identification. Police and soldiers killed the villagers' animals, ate or poisoned their food, stripped their stores of all goods, and burned their clothes.

When the attackers left, four days later, thirty-one village leaders were dead, and the villages were in ruins.

By this time it was deemed wise to remove the McKays and their children. Roland Bunch assumed the responsibilities and the perils of area representative.

Then came what promised to be a dramatic change. In March, 1982, a bloodless coup—effected by a group of young officers who were weary of the continuing corruption—derailed the newly elected regime of General Angel Anibel Guevara and installed General Efrain Rios Montt as president.

Regarded as a moderate, Montt's coming to power, despite its extralegal hue, was acclaimed by a wide array of political leaders—including Marco Vinicio Cerezo Arevalo, the leader of the Christian Democrat Party. A new day, it seemed, had been inaugurated.

The new president wasted little time in stating his priorities and program. Almost four years earlier, he had become a born-again Christian. Though his brother was a bishop in the Catholic Church, Rios Montt had joined a Protestant, charismatic sect called "El Verbo" (the California-based Church of the Complete Word)—one of the many evangelical, charismatic churches springing up throughout Guatemala. Like Teddy Roosevelt, Rios Montt now considered his presidency a "bully pulpit."

In fact, on Sundays—over radio and television—the president delivered sermons to the nation, exhorting all Guatemalans to work for peace—which, he rightly said, begins in the heart. He urged his people to seek justice, not vengeance, and to devote themselves more fully to their families. He called on the men of his country to stop spending their money on liquor and prostitutes.

In his meetings with business leaders, the president called on these executives to recognize that five centuries of "searching for gold" had brought about enormous inequities. He reminded them that 3 million of Guatemala's 7.5 million people earned less than $200 a year. Another 2.5 million made barely $450. The remaining 2 million Guatemalans—who made more than $500 annually—were, he declared, the exploiters of the others.[7]

To lay a foundation for public morality, Rios Montt proposed a three-pronged pledge: "I do not lie"; "I do not steal"; "I do not abuse." By presidential fiat he ordered all military and bureaucratic officials to sign that pledge.

This impressive enactment became a little less inspiring when a local newspaper discovered that 95 percent of its readers didn't believe the pledge would make any difference whatsoever in the behavior of those who took it.

Still, dramatic changes did come about—at least in the metropolitan centers. The streets no longer held their daily quota of slain and mutilated bodies. Citizens could actually enjoy an evening stroll down the broad boulevards. Public officials seemed imbued with a new spirit. "The government," said United States ambassador Chapin, "has come out of the darkness into the light."

But in the Indian highlands it was a different story. Guerilla strength had grown dramatically under the brutality of the Lucas regime. Where once there were only a few hundred, now they numbered thousands. Indians, to whom Marxism-Leninism was a repugnant "unknown tongue," literally fled for their lives from the rampaging security forces, into the arms of the guerillas. Now these augmented bands, flexing their muscles in the face of the new administration, stepped up their deadly provocations.

Something had to be done.

At this point, I had a strong impulse to visit the general himself. I hoped that, by telling him what had been accomplished at Chimaltenango and San Martin, he would come to see more clearly what his people, the highland Indians, really wanted and were capable of achieving. I felt I could exploit a few common denominators. I, too, was a born-again Christian. I, too, had served in the military forces.

But our people in the field felt—and rightly so—that it was far from clear who really held the reins of power in Guatemala. Under such circumstances, exposing our program and personnel more widely could only place them in greater danger.

Reluctantly, I canceled all plans for the trip.

Meanwhile, Rios Montt was becoming increasingly determined to bring the issue to a conclusion. He offered the guerillas two options: dialogue or open warfare. The conditions for dialogue were deemed unacceptable by the guerillas. Warfare ensued.

Unfortunately, guerilla wars are not fought between clearly identified combatants, and "open warfare" came more and more to focus upon the Indian population.

Once again San Martin and the villages of the Chimaltenango District felt its brunt. Hundreds were killed—grandparents, parents, and children. Thousands fled. Livestock were slaughtered. Crops were destroyed. "The army is burning all vegetation," wrote one observer, "from river to river." By the end of 1982, this scorched-earth offensive had destroyed over four hundred Indian villages.

Said the newspaper *El Grafico*, "Massacres have become the order of the day. . . . The kind of genocidal annihilation that is taking place in the Indian zones of the country is truly horrifying."[8]

The regime that had begun with such high promise was winding down in a welter of carnage. Even those who held the general in warm regard—who had acclaimed his elevation and made him the object of their prayers—were forced to conclude that he "either is powerless to stop the rampaging army or he is turning his back on what is happening."[9]

In August, 1983, Rios Montt's regime ended in still another military coup. It placed in the presidential office still another general, Oscar Humberto Mejia Victores.

Under Mejia Victores there was little change in policy or program, with one major exception: He issued a proclamation stating that the military "had no intention of continuing to exercise political influence." In the watershed election of December, 1985, the army deliberately kept hands off, refusing even to endorse the rightist candidate.

So a civilian candidate, attorney Marco Vinicio Cerezo Arevelo, was swept into office with the greatest number of votes in Guatemalan history.

Although one of his first acts was to abolish a police unit accused of long-standing violations of human rights, this was not a signal that a civilian government would now bring wide-scale reform to the military. Many who had directed the massive killings under Lucas Garcia became, in fact, the key figures in organizing the ongoing programs of "pacification." Hundreds have continued to die in the countryside and, to a lesser degree, in the cities. The longed-for progress is agonizingly slow.

Since the election that raised so many hopes and promised so many things—to peasants, students, and labor leaders—there has been a reassertion of power by a coalition of the army and reactionary elements in the private sector. The sunrise of hope still struggles through the night of repression.

At Chimaltenango, our longtime friend, Dr. Carroll Behrhorst, has offered some wise advice:

> Do-good reformers come down here telling the Indians what would be good for them; the guerillas push communism and U.S. reformers push their version of land reform. Nobody bothers to ask the Indians what they want. In fact, the Indians don't want to be "given" anything. They simply want to pay for land and services, and they want to be free to sell their own produce and services. [10]

To me the bloody developments in Guatemala were both harrowing and incredible. For those who were butchered had been, in a sense, my spiritual children. I had helped encourage what had brought them to disaster. That such a thing could happen seemed to make absolutely no sense. After all, to love your neighbor, to do good, to help people, to point the way to better things—this path will insure benediction and invite gratitude. Right?

Wrong. What about Jesus? What about Gandhi? What about Martin Luther King, Jr.?

The brutal fact was that the little band of World Neighbors' worker-teachers had wrought their miracles at the wrong time. They had cast their pearls before the wrong regime. So instead of congratulation, they had reaped condemnation; instead of praise, persecution. Talented personnel had been labeled seditious—and slain. Training programs had become highly suspect—and banned.

Our only option was to take out such personnel as we could and to phase out such programs as we must. But where to turn? And how to proceed?

The answer was in Honduras, where Paul McKay (whose name, we learned, was on a "hit list") had earlier made some excellent contacts. There, in an economy largely distorted by massive infusions of United States military aid, our trained and capable workers, fleeing for their lives, received a warm welcome.

This was largely due to the wisdom and cooperation of Jose Elias Sanchez, a far-sighted member of the Ministry of Natural Resources, who recognized the value of harmonious government and voluntary-agency cooperation and created an instrument to effect such cooperation. It was called ACORDE, and it became our vehicle of operation, with the careful stipulation that basic World Neighbors' principles should prevail in all phases of the program. Rodrigo Castillo Aguilar, the minister of natural resources, gave the enterprise his official blessing.

From all this came a cordial and productive joint operation: "the Integrated Agricultural Development Program of Guinope, El Paraíso, Honduras." Located less than fifty winding miles from

Tegucigalpa, the capital, it brought together two groups that had a common denominator—the experience of poverty. At Guinope, the formerly poor, the Guatemalans, helped the presently poor, the Hondurans.

For the land was miserably unproductive—so much so that it had become a losing venture to attempt to grow crops. Many local farmers, therefore, had rented out their acres as "natural pasture" and traveled miles into the mountains in search of arable plots to cultivate so they could sustain their families. Others had simply given up and moved away. Guinope and its satellite villages were in danger of becoming adobe "ghost towns."

For this very reason, the desolate area seemed an appropriate "restarting base" for our little band of Guatemalan workers. They had fled farms they had built into productive miracles. Now, homesick and handicapped, they received the bleak opportunity to start all over. Honduras had granted them visas. Perhaps this message from Paul McKay also lifted their spirits:

> "It is only natural that you may at first feel a bit sad and strange in this new land. But you must have faith that God is guiding you and preparing you to return to work with your own people one day, when the situation permits.
>
> "In the meantime, it is worthwhile for the extensionists to learn that poverty and hunger have no frontiers and that we need to help our neighbors, wherever we find them. I feel that, in a very special way, God has prepared each one of you for this new mission."

So like a phoenix rising from the ashes, began the new program in Honduras.

The first step was an intensive study. What exactly were the differences in the soils? The rain patterns? The local diseases? The pests? The availability of fertilizer? And what was the most appropriate technology needed to bring about improvement?

Examination showed that years of erosion had left the nearly level land with only about six inches of topsoil. Under this lay an impermeable claypan, which filled with moisture when it rained and left the water-logged topsoil useless.

Our Guatemalan leaders solved this new problem with a system of surface drainage ditches. Once the land was dry, the farmers could plant beans, corn, and coffee. In the months that followed, the corn yield doubled and the bean crop was four times more than local growers had ever gotten before. Moreover, nearly all the coffee trees survived—an unprecedented thing. Field trips, so that other farmers could observe these successes, became the order of the day. The Guatemalans introduced techniques they had already worked with: the incorporation of organic material (green manure, chicken droppings, or compost), the use of contour ditches, and the interchange of experiences.

At first the Guatemalans clung rather closely to one another. But by the time a year had passed, each of them was located in a separate area—surrounded by and training a cadre of Honduran associates. Within five years these associates directed training programs in over 20 communities, involving 211 farm families.

When the Guinope program was six years old, more than three score of these "trainers of trainers" were serving others; twenty-four of them were sought out and given full-time jobs by other agencies, governmental and private. They now reshape training programs throughout Honduras. Some—indoctrinated with the conviction that, having been helped, they were obligated to help others— *walked* to neighboring villages so that they could give two-day and three-day courses on their own.

Moreover, instead of the standard, often inadequate, diet of tortillas and beans, new items began to appear on the tables of the nutrition-conscious women: pies made of Swiss chard and radishes, carrot croquettes, tomato sauce and salads, radish and stuffed-pepper soup, soy milk and its derivatives. There were salads of green corn, bananas, carrots, and oranges and "fruit" drinks of carrots, beets, oranges, lemons, and pineapples. A dietary revolution was underway.

All this did not go unheeded. Wrote Agustin Pio Camey, the project director:

> We continue to receive visits from many other institutions, who come to observe and study the work being done here so that the methods can be transferred to their home areas. The institutions attending are: World Vision, Partners of the Americas, Peace Corps, INA, Pan-American Agricultural School, Catholic Relief Services, APROHCAFE, CARE, FUNDAES, and others.

It should not be a matter of surprise that the Guinope integrated agricultural development program should be chosen by the Honduran government as a national model for agricultural extension work in that needy country. As a result, other centers of operation are underway, with productivity at a level never before achieved.

Success generates emulation. For instance, the reputations established by our Guatemalans in Honduras sparked a search by a number of other development agencies, who began scouring Guatemala in search of anyone who was trained by World Neighbors in soil conservation. Those "alumni" of ours, who have come through the crucible of suffering, are now finding an open door to blessings and benefits.

According to one Honduran official, at least twenty-five agricultural programs—sponsored by other organizations, agencies, or persons—have adopted our pattern of training and technology. In those areas some forty thousand persons are now being reached by these programs. This is real "serendipity."

Not all the Guatemalan worker-teachers joined the flight to Honduras. Some, with their families, made their way north to Mexico and a less than cordial reception.

For Mexico had multiple problems of its own—especially in such hard-pressed states as Oaxaca. The flood of refugees from Guatemala could only aggravate what was already intractable.

As I learned of this desperate exodus, I recalled my visit to Mexico, almost twenty years earlier. With some of my staff, we had visited the Mesquital, a barren waste whose stony expanse was relieved here and there by an improbable village. Though only a two-hour drive from Mexico City, it seemed continents removed.

A concerned indigenous group—mostly clerics and professional people—had invited us to join in a ministry to the hundreds of people who lived like timorous animals in the rocks and crannies of that arid tract. We were inclined to try.

But delays and difficulties—mostly bureaucratic ones—beset our path. Some of those "difficulties" were justified. For Mexico already directed an abundance of public and private service agencies and groups, all of which intended to produce basic social improvement.

Therefore we could understand if that nation's overstressed bureaucracy rolled out no red carpet for well-meaning *Norte Americanos* who came with one more offer of help. At any rate, we did not go further with our relationship.

Now, in early 1981, we had an investment in love and concern that overrode all our earlier hesitancies. The question was not would we help but, simply, how? How could our Guatemalan trainees be transformed from unwanted refugees to welcomed agents of productive change?

The answer seemed to lie in our motto: "Go where the need is the greatest and the workers are the fewest." In Mexico that meant the area of Yodcono, one of the poorest sections of the poorest state in Mexico—Oaxaca. First of all, the soil the desperate villagers attempted to cultivate was in what seemed the final stages of erosion. Our Guatemalans knew some remedial answers. Second, the whole area was earthquake prone, with people still sharply aware of the damage done the previous October. Our experience in the construction of tremor-resistant structures would minister to a keenly felt need.

But there were problems. Despite a common Mayan heritage, Mexican practices and attitudes often differed widely from those of the Guatemalans. The early going was rough.

At the end of two years, however, farmers produced from five to fifteen times as much beans and corn (the basic staples throughout Central America) as they had ever produced before. The barren land had become alive and productive.

This meant two things. Exodus to the urban slums ceased. Escape—as illegal emigrants to the United States—was no longer necessary. Farmers who *had* left, learning of the new developments, returned to their ancestral acres.

In brief, the once beleaguered Guatemalans have transmitted to their Mexican associates what they themselves learned back in Chimaltenango. In turn, the Mexican leaders—increasing in numbers, confidence, and ability—pass those same lessons on to *their* friends and neighbors. It is the contagious teaching that real self-help is *possible*, that *you* can do it, that it *will change your life*, and that it requires that you *share it with others*.[11]

In Mexico—aswirl with political and economic problems—a tug-of-war continues between two policies. One is to keep urban food prices so low that domestic turbulence will be unlikely. The other is to somehow permit farmers, who make up about 40 percent of the population, to make a living. For farmers will not—indeed, cannot—provide food that they must sell at a loss.

Even if that issue could be resolved, there is little, if any, land left to distribute to campesinos and their growing families. This means that they *must* learn to produce more on what they now have, find ways of restoring land that has become arid, and begin the practice of family planning.

A Mexico built "from the bottom up" can have a glorious tomorrow.

7

Stalking the Elusive Greenback

For every month I spent overseas, involved with projects, I had to spend three in the United States and Canada, involved with problems. Those problems were all alike—how do we pay for the spreading program? Some nights I woke up in a cold sweat, having dreamed that I was on an overloaded cockleshell, headed straight for the rocks. If the dream seemed nightmarish, the reality was scarcely less. *Why*, I thought, *is it so hard to raise money for something that does so much good?*

Part of the answer was that we had hedged ourselves about with so many restraints. We had decided, for instance, that we would not accept government subsidy. This had not been easy. Some months earlier, I had been invited to Washington to meet with the acting director of Point Four (now called the Agency for International Development). He had looked into our work and liked what he saw.

"I'm impressed," he told me, "and I'll tell you how I feel. We're the bureaucrats. You're the people. I'm going to take some of these millions we've got and give them to you."

I couldn't believe my ears. *This can't be real*, I thought. *It's got to be a dream.*

It wasn't a dream; it was a mirage. For our legal staff speedily made it clear that, if we accepted those millions, we would be subject to direction and review not only by our own officialdom but also by their opposite numbers in those countries where we would serve. By that time we had had the opportunity to see how such programs were more likely to produce dependence than liberation.

This aimed at precisely the opposite of our intended goal. We wanted to encourage indigenous responsibility, indigenous pride, indigenous leadership. Besides, I wanted to be able to challenge our prospective associates in the villages of the Third World to meet our contribution with theirs, our sacrifices with their own. Somehow I felt such a challenge would ring false and prove impotent in an aura of government support and bureaucratic involvement. The directors agreed, so we turned down the generous offer.

Moreover, moved by a costly fastidiousness, we had made two other decisions that did anything but enhance our ability as fund-raisers. First, we decided that, as a "developmental" enterprise, we would not feature starving babies. I had been appalled as I had visited the work of a sister agency and watched mothers, in their rags, cringe as they and their dying children were photographed and photographed and photographed. Second, we held real reservations about opting for the sponsor-a-child strategy. It seemed to us that jeopardized normal and necessary family relationships. *In what position does this leave parental authority? Or the other children?* we wondered. We also had real questions about its cost accountability, since it is far cheaper to teach a father or mother to do the things that improve health and increase income than it is to continue to funnel monthly support to some "sponsored" child.

Yet, as everyone knows, by these tactics millions of dollars are readily raised. Others tapped into this cornucopia; why shouldn't we?

We just didn't.

But what *could* we do?

About this time an acquaintance who was aware of our plight and who "knew his way around" on the slippery slopes of financial accounting said he had just the answer we were looking for.

"There are lots of businesses—in the fields of food products, seeds, and drugs—who would love to give an organization like yours some substantial gifts from time to time."

He explained that they could charge the gifts off as charitable donations and oftentimes come out better than if they put them on the market.

"You, on the other hand, can then send those gifts overseas. It's all on the up-and-up. You're feeding people, checking diseases, and planting crops. It will let you show small administrative costs and big program outlays. It's the perfect answer you're looking for."

So it seemed—until we began to note that too many of the gifts arrived just as the dates of their wholesomeness, potency, and—of course—salability were about to expire. By the time they arrived at their overseas destination, they were virtually worthless. They *did* provide the voluntary agency a chance to submit an attractive annual report, and they did enable some of the donor companies to take a tax write-off, instead of a loss. In fact, everybody seemed to win except the needy villager, the unsuspecting public, and the Internal Revenue Service (for whom it's difficult to become lachrymose).

At any rate we decided to look every commodity "gift horse" carefully in the mouth. Too many of them had poor teeth and bad breath.

But we began to feel like Mother Hubbard. Our cupboard was growing increasingly bare. In turning down the government funds and rejecting surefire appeals, we felt we had acted on principle. But principle, however noble, pays no salaries, buys no plows, provides no seed, and supplies no fertilizer.

It was, we all agreed, time to call in the professionals. So we invited to our headquarters the representatives of five of the major reputable fund-raising organizations in the country. They examined our literature, looked at our program, and heard our queries. Then most of them threw up their hands.

"We raise money," said one, "for hospitals, churches, peace movements, and natural disasters. You people are talking about 'development'—a long-term, insubstantial concept. If that is what we have to work with, we can't say, as we do when we're raising funds for a hospital, 'You had better give, for you don't know when *you* may need this service.'

"You don't have members. So we can't put pressure—as in the case of a church or college—on some parishioner or alumnus and ask him to 'lean on' somebody else. Why, you're not even talking about starving children! You've left out all the good parts—the pathos, the emotion. Frankly, you're not the kind of organization fund-raisers get in line for. I just don't see how my agency can help you." Three of the remaining four echoed his sentiments.

The last one was more encouraging. As the meeting drew to its close, he pushed back his chair and said, "I like what you're doing. I believe I can help you. Why don't you come by my office and see if we can't develop a campaign?"

We met with him—in an office filled with banks of mailing lists. He explained how he worked. It all sounded great—until he stated his fee. At that point we parted company. Using his services would have bankrupted us in three months.

Back in our headquarters—and back on our haunches—we tried to take stock. The "doctors" had spoken. Unless we changed the character of our program, we couldn't survive.

Then came the letter from the Fund for Asia.

This fund, according to its prospectus, did not intend to become an operating agency with projects of its own. Instead it would assist other agencies that, in their judgment, were worthy of such aid. They had screened forty-eight organizations that were undertaking projects in Asia and had chosen twelve to whom they were going to render assistance. World Neighbors was one of the twelve. We were asked to submit a reasonable request for aid—which, of course, we did.

As I read their lovely letter, I could scarcely believe my eyes: Their "development officer" was the same fund-raiser whose services we had reluctantly foregone!

Several weeks later, we were invited to attend the kick-off dinner, in the ballroom of the Waldorf Astoria. *It's really true*, I marveled as I sat looking at the ambassadors from Asia who graced the head table and listening to the eloquent remarks of Henry Grady and James Michener (who was president of the fund), *God* does *work in mysterious ways his wonders to perform. Here is this tried and proven fund-raiser whom we couldn't afford. And now, God—with James Michener as his agent—is giving him to us. Hallelujah!*

I misread Providence. The Fund for Asia—for all its good intentions and obvious expertise—was unable to transmute high promise into hard cash. We had asked for $75,000. After two years, we received $1,500. Then the fund folded. It was a sad hour.

It was also a long trip and a rough landing as we came back from cloud nine to square one. Maybe the "experts" were right. Maybe we *were* the sort of program you can't raise money for. Gloom filled my soul.

Now, when Jesus faced his tempter in the wilderness, he knew which satanic offers to refuse. When Bunyan's Christian was on his way to the Celestial City, he knew what deceptive detours to avoid. I didn't, and my only excuse was that legitimate needs were crying out so loud, I couldn't hear the warning bells.

For instance, news reached me one day that a remarkable financier would be interested in using some of his corporate billions in helping World Neighbors extend its overseas projects. He was, my informant assured me, a man with a real concern for "little people." In fact, his financial empire had grown out of his determination to open up the rewarding field of mutual funds to the small investor. Now he wanted to go further—to reach out to the world's *really* poor. Our program of helping people to help themselves strongly appealed to him.

Conversations and correspondence followed the initial appointment. But nothing followed the correspondence. Though I didn't know it, we had reached him about the time his fifty thousand stockholders were clamoring for his hide. It was no time for him to be considering new benevolences.

Besides, Bernie Cornfeld had changed dramatically from his Eagle Scout days back in Brooklyn, New York. Investors Overseas Services had become, according to one of its officers, "a monster which devoured its creators." To have won its patronage would have brought all the benefits of a first-class reservation on the Titanic.

Even when—through such prosaic procedures as letters, lectures, speeches, and sermons—we had begun to build a donor base of hundreds, I still kept looking for that corporate "angel" who would chauffeur us to El Dorado. That is why my ears pricked up one afternoon when an enthusiastic acquaintance burst into my office.

"John," he said, perched on the edge of his seat and speaking with a verve that would have delighted Pat Sajak, "I know exactly the man you need to see. In three years he's built a program from nothing to more than a hundred million dollars. Now he's getting ready to go international with a new program called "Dare to Be Great." He had to drop out of school at an early age, and he started life with a harelip. So he's especially interested in helping people who have been bypassed or handicapped. He talks all the time—just like you— about how much better it is to *teach* a man to fish than just to *give* him a fish. I believe he would grab World Neighbors like a duck grabs a June bug.

"He's terribly busy, but I know him and I believe he'd find time to talk with you if you can get by to see him. He lives in Orlando, and I'll be glad to put in a word for you. What do you say?"

The whole thing sounded providential. I was just getting ready to leave for a series of engagements in Florida. Going by Orlando would be no problem at all. I didn't even hesitate. "Sure. Write him or call him. I'd love to meet him. Here's my schedule."

A few weeks later, following a meeting in Jupiter, Florida, I called the offices of Koscot Interplanetary and talked to an executive secretary. She had heard from my friend and wanted me to know that her boss would have been glad to see me but that he had been called away for some pressing meetings in New York and Washington. Could I get back with them, perhaps in early summer?

I said I would try.

But things began to go awry for Glenn Turner. He had seen the world, perhaps even the universe, as his oyster. But the tool he used to open that oyster—"pyramid selling" of franchises—brought him under nationwide attack. District attorneys from more than forty states initiated lawsuits against him. He was indicted in Michigan and Florida for conspiracy to cheat and defraud. And he faded from the national scene after spending years—and most of his money—in and out of the courts.

Well-intentioned though he may have been, we might have wound up in the arid reaches of outer space had we hitched our wagon to this erratic star.

I decided once more that we should stick to our knitting. As we did, we made progress—noteworthy but not sensational, gratifying but not intoxicating. I still felt it was not enough.

Two years passed. Then came the call from California. A man with a doctor's degree and significant experience with a governmental program overseas spoke, his first words apulse with excitement: "Listen, John. There's a man out here you've just got to meet. He's a little unorthodox, but he's got a ministry to people that's both unusual and effective—and he's got influence you wouldn't believe. I think he could help you."

I asked probing questions. He gave approving answers.

"But if you're going to catch him," he insisted, "you've got to move fast. I understand he's been given *carte blanche* to set up a self-help program somewhere in Latin America. He'll be leaving for there within the next few days. Give him a ring," he gave me the phone number. "I'm sure he'd like to know about some of the things you've been doing. Who knows, you two might join up together."

I thanked him, promised to check it out, said good-bye and hung up. But when I repeatedly tried to reach the number given me, I kept getting a busy signal. Finally, the operator told me the phone was off the hook.

So I wrote to this dynamic leader at his post-office box in Redwood Valley. A few weeks later I received a letter from his secretary, who sent cordial words from her boss and enclosed a brochure.

There was a convalescent home, "Hilltop Haven"; "Happy Acres Boys' Ranch"; most of all, there was "The People's Temple," in Los Angeles—with a caravan of buses that "spread the Good News of Spiritual Healing and Human Service Ministry."

It was a warm letter and an impressive layout, but it failed to suggest a time and place when this remarkable leader and I could get together.

Too bad, I thought as I filed the correspondence away—not realizing that we had escaped involvement in an authoritarian ministry that left Jim Jones and his hundreds of followers in bloody windrows on the floor of a "tabernacle" in Guyana.

But though my appeals for the $30,000 needed in Indonesia had received a rebuff from the various "committees" of People to People, they had not fallen on wholly deaf ears. One day there appeared in my office a quiet young man who assured me his agency was ready to help. "We can supply the $30,000 you say you need, and there will be nothing on the public record and no expectation of repayment. But we, too, have workers in Indonesia. All we would ask is this: If the time came when it seemed expedient to *move* one of them for a time, we would expect the right to merge him into your operation in the Philippines."

A red flag popped up in my mind. I knew a number of private agencies had accepted CIA support. The advancement of free-world interests, they felt, justified the action, and we needed the money as a hemophiliac needs blood. But we didn't want plasma that might carry a latent infection. It really wasn't hard for me to say no.

Not all of my pursuits had such a *Perils of Pauline* quality. Some smacked more of *Saturday Night Live*. A friend of mine, for instance, had secured an interview for me with a very wealthy man who was, I was told, "fighting Communism." He should, thought my friend, therefore be inclined to help World Neighbors. I agreed. So punctually at the appointed hour, I opened the door to his outer office.

It was sumptuously appointed, with exotic nudes covering the wallpaper. I must confess I felt self-conscious and embarrassed when I introduced myself to the attractive receptionist. As she led me into the inner sanctum, I expected to meet a real "swinger."

So the man's first question almost floored me: "Peters," said the rough-hewn character, never bothering to rise from his chair, "do you believe the Bible from cover to cover?"

I pulled up my chair in front of his desk and replied that I did.

"Do you believe anybody who doesn't can be a Christian and make it to heaven?"

"Well," I replied, "there's coming a day when the sheep will be divided from the goats. They call it the Judgment Day. The Bible says the Son of man will decide who makes it and who doesn't. I think I'll leave that question of yours up to Him."

He didn't like that answer, and he let me know it by pounding on his desk. "Well," he bellowed with a blistering curse, "there's just them that is and them that ain't!"

From that point on, our conversation went downhill. He learned I was a Methodist—"You've all been brainwashed." He discovered I had been to Yale—"You've got to be a pinko." He looked at the brochure I had given him—"How do I know it's not a Communist front?"

I'd had about enough. Besides I had a rather solid feeling that this man was not going to become a major donor to World Neighbors. So I stood up.

"Look," I said, "we're wasting each other's time. I think we both have better things to do. So I'll say good-bye and be on my way."

With that he got out of his chair, walked around his desk, put his arm across my shoulders, and accompanied me to the door. "Peters," he said, "I like you."

I thought for a moment, as we walked past his erotic wallpaper, that he might break down and make a contribution to our program. But he never did.

Others, however, came forward to take his place. For we were beginning to receive a certain amount of publicity. Milwaukee's Merle and Frank Sinclair had produced a beautifully done piece for the *Saturday Evening Post*. It had been titled "Look What This Preacher Started," and more than a few people read it. The Sinclairs, whom I came to know and love, were high in my galaxy of stars.

I was even given a few minutes on the *Today* show—though Dave Garroway insisted that we only mimicked CARE. Art Linkletter was much more responsive when he had me on *House Party*. Bob Considine extended an invitation for me to meet him at Toots Shor's. Yogi Berra had said that this famous bistro was "so crowded nobody goes there anymore." So I arrived a few minutes early and was shown to the table reserved for just such meetings. The irrepressible Toots drifted over.

"You've got to be a celebrity," he boomed, "or you wouldn't be sitting *here*. What do you do?"

It was a perfect opening, and I told him all about our work, not missing an opportunity to point out how much more we could do if he chose to help us. He chose instead to regale me with an uproarious account of an evening down south (he couldn't quite place my accent) when he had had a few too many, climbed up on a table, fell off, and broke his leg. As Toots told it, it was a good story. But I didn't know what to do with it or where to go from there. Fortunately Considine saved the day by arriving and getting enough information from me for two deeply appreciated columns.

I suppose it's a natural law that one thing leads to another. What else? At any rate, after we received a sensitive write-up in *Guideposts*, Lowell Thomas got in touch with me. He had apparently been assured by Dr. Norman Vincent Peale—or by *Guideposts* editor Len LeSourd—that I was "all right." So he asked if I could speak to the Dutch Treat Club, a group of New York's creative writers, editors, directors, and media people. He named a date, and I arranged to be there.

It was an occasion that called for a virtuoso performance. And I, just beginning to come down with the flu (though I didn't yet know it), fell far short. Nevertheless, though no funds had been mentioned or solicited, one quietly smiling, famous man pushed through the departing company and insisted on making a gift to our program.

It was not, however, the famous or the wealthy who became the real day-after-day supporting sinews of World Neighbors. We were grateful for their endorsements and gifts. There were times when we could not have survived without these "super donors" and the occasional grants extended by those foundations that recognized the crucial need for "development."

But when Clarence Hall's article, "Neighbors to All the World," appeared in *Reader's Digest*, we found that it was people—just warmhearted, good, sensitive people—who would become the flesh and blood of our movement.

I found these lovely folks in homes, offices, civic clubs, and churches across the United States and Canada: teachers, business people, laborers, executives, mothers, fathers, widows, and children—the salt of the earth.

At first I had a real hesitancy in asking them for help. Most were far from affluent. But one of my hard-nosed advisers had said, "John, the only money you'll ever get is the money you ask for. And you've got to make it clear that you can't do this job with mirrors."

So I asked, and they gave—the nurse in North Carolina, who had wanted to be a missionary; the families in Ohio, who sent contributions instead of Christmas cards; the young people in Illinois, who gave up their vacation time to work for World Neighbors; the heiress who poured out her bounty so generously; the Future Homemakers of America, who collected their dimes and quarters; the widow who fasted; and the pensioner who shared.

As they gave, they said, "Thank you for letting me have a part in this ministry. . . . " "I'll look on this as an investment in neighborliness. . . . " "You are helping not just the underprivileged but also those of us who are so overprivileged. . . . " "Thank you for letting us enrich our own lives as we do for others. . . ." "You are capitalizing on the qualities that made this nation great. . . . " "This is a program to make humans glad they are humans."

From a military hospital, lads recovering from serious wounds wrote, "This is the kind of army I really want to enlist in; this is the kind of war I really want to fight."

These words, to an ex-chaplain, were soul stirring. And I thanked God that the temptation to give up, so often at my elbow, had never reached my heart.

I grasped hope like a newly sharpened sword and went forth to slay once more the dragons of discouragement.

8

Return to the
Southern Hemisphere

As a loyal supporting base expanded and as a headquarters staff increased in numbers and improved in competence I once again assumed my overseas itineration. The major lodestone this time was South America.

I made trips in pirogues, down the roiling rivers of Colombia; spine-jarring journeys into the Brazilian interior; I had wintry meetings with warm friends in the Bolivian Andes; conferences with tribal co-ops in Ecuador; made muddy treks to new fishponds in Paraguay. Gradually I became better acquainted with my hemispheric neighbors.

But Peru caught and held me. We landed, Orm Greene and I, at the old port city of Callao and pushed our way through eight miles of unrestrained motorized pandemonium. I was almost overwhelmed by this vehicular menagerie. Cars, trucks, and buses of every conceivable description flocked to the roadway. Some free-lance buses and taxis, called "collectivos," consisted of components of such ancient vintage and divergent origin that "identification" was impossible. But, amazingly, they kept running—pausing once in a while at street corners as passengers scampered on and tumbled off.

No question about it, Lima was alive!

In the succeeding days I had conferences with the Roy Smiths (of the Peruvian YMCA), civic officials, business managers, social workers, church leaders, expatriates, and others. There were visits to the *barriadas* and reports from the jungle. We reviewed progress and considered prospects.

The problems of Lima itself were mind-boggling. Population in 1965 (the time of my arrival) was around 2 million and climbing (it had been 528,000 in 1948). Although it was a lovely city of cathedrals, museums, and universities, a collar of 163 slum communities —with a population of .5 million—throttled it. More people were coming.

The process both fascinated and dismayed me. Groups of migrants, desperate for a chance to make a living, would come in from the mountains or the jungles and stay, for a time, with relatives who had preceded them. Then, at some prearranged hour—usually at around 1:00 to 3:00 A.M.—they would come together on a vacant piece of ground and establish a new community.

By the time the authorities discovered them, "homes" had been erected—four large stakes driven into the ground and wrapped around with woven mats. Later the makeshift *barriada* would become a *pueblo jovenes*, "new town," with homes made of mud brick and flattened oil tins.

With the settlement a fait accompli, the overburdened city would extend what services it could. But sanitation was generally nonexistent, and water had to be brought in by truck. Nutrition was poor and sickness rife.

So we tried to help, working with other agencies to get water piped in and doing what we could to provide public health nurses, improved sanitation, classes in nutrition, and courses in productive enterprise.

Gradually these human dumping grounds improved. Some even became attractive. Yet this, we began to see, was *not* what should be happening. For, to the campesino with too many children and too little land, the *barriada*, with all its faults and filth, was *already* attractive. To make it more so, while nothing was done to improve the *campo*, "fields," simply increased the migration from the countryside and multiplied the overburdened city's problems.

Instead we felt we needed to help maintain the barest essentials in the *barriadas* and to bend every effort toward making the village more attractive. Our job was to restore the soil, not abandon it; to deal with the underlying problem, not with its erupting symptoms. We needed to go to the mountains and jungles.

In the jungles, working with the Summer Institute of Linguistics, we began a program that offered a wide range of developmental projects to the tribes who wanted them and appeared ready to cope with them. We introduced portable sawmills; established a revolving-loan program; trained people in the use of new tools and machinery, in poultry growing, upbreeding of livestock; and we helped them purchase large motors, making profitable river trade and travel possible. A careful process of supervision and follow-up was built into the program. Perhaps for this reason we received such punctual repayments that in the first six years the $15,000 revolving fund had "turned over" a sufficient number of times to make 300 significant loans to 16 different Indian tribes in the Peruvian jungles.

Within the next few years, this program increased dramatically. For the tribes—assisted by their SIL counselors—organized new communities, started new industries, built their own stores, operated their own river transport, sold their own produce (rice, beans, coffee, honey, bananas, peanuts, cocoa, and rubber), and financed their own programs of civic improvement. Their incomes more than doubled, and they came to the happy realization that they need not be destroyed by advancing "civilization"; they could successfully compete with the white man and still retain what was of value in their own culture.

Landmark legislation was passed, providing for the recognition of Indian communities and the issuance of title for Indian lands— something never done before. Over the next five years, land titles to more than 89,000 acres were completed and signed—a major advance in the status of communities once regarded as the lairs of savages and headhunters.

We were, of course, pleased and gratified with the progress of the tribes along the Amazon—the Agaruna, Shipibo, Machiguenga, Ticuna, Yarapaga, and others. But we were becoming aware of even deeper needs among the 4 million Quechua—descendants of the once-mighty Incas—who eked out a miserable existence in one of the world's most inhospitable environments, the high reaches of the Peruvian Andes.

"You simply can't believe how they live," said a local social worker. "Ninety percent of them have never been more than three miles from the place they were born. They are suspicious of each other and deadly afraid of outsiders. Those who live on the huge, mountainous haciendas are virtual slaves—told by the owners that, if they try to escape, the evil spirits will pursue and devour them.

"Those who live 'free' often dwell in caves and holes that are so filthy I wouldn't put my pigs in them. When they get paid, they receive one sol a day—which is around four cents. It's almost a hopeless prospect."

Obviously, if we were to go where "the need is the greatest and the workers are the fewest," the Andean villages were our target. We wondered if anyone could break through the wall of apprehension and direct the needed programs of development and self-help.

There was such a man. His name was Saul Lamberto, and he was a Peruvian agronomist whose early years had been spent among the Quechua. Saul had also become a committed Christian, and he saw service to others as a natural and necessary expression of his faith. Our friends in the Summer Institute of Linguistics called him to our attention, and we felt fortunate when he agreed to be our representative in this pioneering venture.

Saul could have made his headquarters in the relatively comfortable villages near the city of Huancayo, which even boasted a university. But he pushed on into the unfriendly highlands, finally stopping at the little village of Cuchokisera, in the township of Quispillagat. It lay in the department called Ayacucho, "the corner of death," and it deserved that name. For this was the lowest-income-per-capita area in Peru. Malnutrition, disease, and high infant mortality were its hallmarks.

Saul came into the village on horseback, dressed just as the villagers dressed, speaking Quechua. But in his equipment he carried a camera (for taking color slides), a small but powerful projector (which World Neighbors distributes worldwide), and a tape recorder. In the years to come, these would be his "visual aids" in the teaching program that would spread across the rugged mountainsides.

The village, he found, depended upon the raising of sheep for its livelihood. The animals, living entirely on the thin natural pasture, were the primary sources of food and clothing. The villagers also raised an ever-diminishing crop of barley and potatoes.

Life was grim: Income was around fifty dollars a year, and conditions were worsening. About a fourth of the lambs died every year, either from parasites or from the calamitous changes in the often-freezing temperature. The soil was becoming less and less productive, the pastures less and less nourishing.

After a period of getting acquainted, learning local mores, and winning confidence, Saul began to talk with the village leader, Salomon Galindo. He suggested the pastures could and should be improved. Salomon was dumbfounded.

"The idea seemed ridiculous," he later said. "I was convinced that pastures just grow—all by themselves. Nature makes the decision as to what will grow or not grow. And our animals must simply make out with what they are given."

But Saul persisted. "I know a man who is an expert on pastures," he said. "He's with a Swiss technical mission here in the Andes. Let me see if I can get him to come and talk with you and the rest of the village. When you've heard him, you can make up your minds."

The villagers, skeptical and suspicious, finally agreed. The "expert" came. He told them about a new kind of grass that actually needed frost to grow and develop. With that, many of the villagers felt sure that he was crazy.

But Salomon now trusted Saul, and this news intrigued him. He agreed to let his land be planted to the new grass seed, even fencing it in to protect it from roving animals.

"Time passed slowly," he reported. "Finally the first shoots appeared, astonishing my family and the community. Then the grass began to grow—thick and green. Within three months the grass was tall enough to cut, and for the first time that year my animals had the privilege of a juicy green dinner. Because my land had a spring on it, I had grass all year long, even during the drought.

"Now I go to bed each night to dream peacefully of the present and the future."

This began a remarkable change for the villages of the Altiplano. Sheep grew and fattened. Improved rams were brought in to upgrade the flocks. Sheep dips were built to control the parasites. Wool yields quadrupled—and so did income. The new grass grew so abundantly the sheep could not consume it all.

Next the villagers tried a new cattle-fattening project. In April they arranged a loan and bought ten bulls, weighing an average of 650 pounds, for thirteen cents a pound. The bulls were fed the nutritious mixed grasses. Early in July the villagers sold the fattened animals, which averaged 770 pounds, for twenty cents a pound!

After paying back their loan and deducting all expenses, they found that they had made $424—a huge amount in that poor area.

All this time Saul assiduously recorded the improvements and testimonials on slides and tape. Carrying the "before" and "after" color pictures of crops and livestock and the message of the amazing benefits—told by recognizable voices of their neighbors—from village to village, he spread a startling and convincing propaganda. With others, whom he persuaded to be his "assistant country agents," he took the news of transformation throughout the area. Besides that he offered a new kind of barley, potatoes, and corn—all of which added greatly to nutrition and income.

This was done in spite of almost impassable roads and in the midst of almost impossible weather. For aspiration gradually replaced suspicion. What one village had done, the others could emulate.

At the end of four years Saul Lamberto felt he had accomplished his task in that area. His message had spread from one small hamlet to scores of others. The number of families who had been helped had increased from a few dozen to over 7,000. The project was almost self-multiplying.

He now knew that the once poor, frightened, suspicious people of the village could determine their own destiny. The door to the future had been opened, and they were entering.

So with our blessings and thanks, Saul moved to another needy village on the Altiplano—Cepropampa, 130 kilometers away by car and an additional 40 kilometers by mule train.

We could afford his move, for we had, by this time, acquired an Andean area representative for all our projects in Peru and Bolivia. He was, and is, Edward Ruddell who, with his wife Pilar, guides some of the most dramatic developments in our hemisphere.

Ed, who came to us in 1971, has a master's degree in agricultural economics. Before joining World Neighbors, he was a team member and, later, director of the American Friends Service Committee programs in Mexico. He continues to nourish, encourage, and provide overall counsel to projects throughout the Altiplano.

He was present when Development Alternatives (commissioned by USAID) chose the program centered at Cuchokisera—just as they had chosen the World Neighbors project in San Martin, Guatemala—as one of forty-one locally based development projects to be included in their worldwide study. When they completed that two-year study, Cuchokisera was classified as "number five" (San Martin was named "number one").

"It is worth noting," their report points out, "that 75 percent of the population of Cuchokisera are 'reborn Christians,' who do not smoke, drink, or chew cocoa." More had been at work than the mere transmission of technical skills.

Later, Dr. Robert Stickney—who had served with AID, WHO, and the International Rice Institute of the Philippines—pronounced *his* judgment. He called the Cuchokisera-centered operation "the best program I have ever seen."

Not surprisingly, as he continues the supervision of the Andean area project, Ed has received a large number of citations and awards from various agencies of the government of Peru.

All the Peruvian programs have included family planning as one component. In Lima itself, doctors and nurses, with our help, offer services at approximately one hundred health centers in the "young towns" and throughout the slum areas. Among the jungle tribes, family planning is increasingly sought (though one tribe already had its answer in a drug they had discovered but had not shared). In the Andes, where desperate mothers simply let unwanted babies die, we have enlisted doctors and midwives to minister to the need.

We feel obligated to do this, since benefits come primarily to those who suffer most in the Third World: the women of the lower classes. It is their cause Pilar Ruddell, Ed's wife, has made her own.

In order to provide income for this group—and to increase their sense of self-worth—Pilar has organized a Women's Handicraft Cooperative, with headquarters in one of Lima's "new towns." Its members, who call themselves *Los Pilares*, first underwent a training program in organizational methods and in the improvement of knitting and weaving skills. They now sell handicrafts locally and abroad. The returns have enabled each of them to set up a savings account and to acquire a much-needed degree of independence.

Not long ago the president of the board paid Pilar a deserved tribute. "Without your constant support," she said, "our cooperative would never have been formed. Your confidence and faith in our abilities were just what we needed. We have always been seen as ignorant women, uneducated and therefore useless to society. But the cooperative has changed our lives. This is why we are so grateful and hope that you can continue helping us, because we have only just started the battle."

One part of that battle will be a reduction in the birth rate—an eventuality that almost always follows when an increasing number of women find income-producing occupation.

Only a Pollyanna would assume that all Peru's problems are nearly solved. If progress has been made in one area, a major challenge has erupted in another. It is called *Sendero Luminoso*, "the Shining Path." Marxism, Mao style, is its creed. Violence, Pol Pot variety, is its tactic. Feeding on indigenous poverty, governmental ineptitude, and the expanding drug traffic, it is a major threat to Peruvian stability.

The idea for the Shining Path began in the mid 1960s in the classroom of Abimael Guzman, a philosophy professor at the University of Huamanga in Ayacucho City. He had become enamored of the teachings of Mao, convinced that deliverance from injustice and inequity must come by the direct involvement of the indigenous population. Where better to start than in the poverty-blasted district of Ayacucho? Impassioned and convincing, he gathered a band of student followers about him.

In time, these followers, immersing themselves in Quechua language and customs, penetrated the countryside. Working mostly undercover, they became teachers and organizers. Always before them was the pattern set by the Cultural Revolution in China and the Khmer Rouge in Cambodia. As evangels of a new religion, they sought and won hundreds of converts. As armed guerillas, they demanded cooperation, brutally executing those who refused it. Since they began their bloody forays, thousands in Peru's villages and cities have died.

One fall evening in 1982, eighteen of the Sendero Luminoso, their machine guns hidden in gunnysacks, entered Cuchokisera. They went directly to the home of the Galindo brothers, Salomon and Teofilo. These two were widely recognized as the resident leaders of the World Neighbors–assisted program. For over three hours the guerillas threatened, queried, and brutalized the Galindos. At the end of that time, they passed judgment: The brothers must die.

"You've opened the door to these foreigners who have come to exploit the people," they intoned. "You don't deserve to live any longer."

But the villagers had learned of their presence. In no uncertain terms, they let the guerillas know that, if they killed the Galindos, the entire area would be up in arms against them. They made it clear that they were *not* exploited, that the leadership was, and had been, their own people.

The guerillas, persuaded almost against their will, finally withdrew. One, particularly impressed by the villagers' testimonies, suggested that the training might be extended to his area and people, once "the revolution" had succeeded in taking over the government—which they expect to do by 1990.

During the succeeding months the devout villagers made it a point to include these guerillas in their prayers. Two years later, at a youth camp, some of the younger members of the Sendero Luminoso decided to become Christians. They did not announce that decision to their comrades, but a year later, at a second such "camp," they brought some of their friends with them. The "good infection," as C. S. Lewis called it, appears to be spreading.

Just what difference this may make in the overall picture is still a question. For as the military—whose soldiers are almost completely unacquainted with the Andean villagers—have pursued the guerillas, they have killed enough innocent people to alienate large sectors of the countryside. But amid all this, the Galindo brothers have witnessed a remarkable phenomenon. Though they have carefully separated their evangelical witness from their development teachings, they have seen—in the very midst of this bloody persecution—twelve new churches formed, with some 4,000 newly converted and baptized members. During that same time, the development program itself has spread from eight to sixty-eight communities.

A much greater expansion is in prospect. Six new training centers have just been established, with campesinos walking for eight miles or more through rugged mountain passes just for the privilege of learning the new, liberating lessons. Meanwhile the dramatic changes that have come to this once-wretched corner of Peru have received the approval and encouragement of officials in the Ministry of Agriculture, the Ministry of Education, and the Ministry of External Affairs. These agencies have been especially pleased that we gave support and authority to local indigenous leadership. The accomplishments of such leadership amaze them.

The good news continues to spread. Through field trips, seminars, conferences, educational television, and scientific journals, the character and progress of these programs have received wide publicity. Official "agreements" have been signed, comprehensive plans completed, and major progress is anticipated—*provided* sufficient funding and qualified personnel become available.

So, at present, the program operates under its own indigenous directors as *Vecinos Peru,* "Neighbors Peru." It is committed to the proposition that all its members must strive for full self-reliance—no longer dependent on the state, on patrons, or on outside organizations. This we applaud and encourage. We are, of course, pleased to retain our relationship as devoted friends, counselors, and—if need be—facilitators.

9

High-Level High Jinks

"Why don't you people get together?" asked the overdriven home minister of a Third World country plaintively. "You're the fourth representative of a relief agency to see me this week. I don't want to be rude, but I really don't have time for all of you—at least separately."

His question missed a fact and made a point: We weren't a "relief" agency, but we were a time-consuming interruption.

This conviction weighed on me. *Why don't agencies that have programs of similar or related purpose establish some kind of "command post" where information can be shared, projects correlated, administrative costs lessened, and trips like this reduced?* I thought. For we were in a battle—against poverty on one hand and apathy on the other. We needed some kind of jointly shared "war room" where we could sort out our priorities, take concerted action on our procedures, and even decide on times and tactics for approaching the public.

Each group, I realized, had its distinctive body of donors, and none was ready to open its carefully cultivated pastures for common grazing. These were real hurdles. Still, the goal seemed worth pursuing.

But I felt convinced that the only way we could wrangle such skittish mavericks into a common corral was to have the invitation issued by someone whose motives were too dispassionate to suspect and whose credentials were too impressive to ignore. Who in the world met those criteria?

I talked the matter over with the chairman of my board, W. E. Chope, the founder of Industrial Nucleonics. "Why don't you ask President Eisenhower?" he said. "He could, if he wanted to, call it a White House Conference."

It seemed the ideal answer.

We began corresponding with some of the president's aides— Bryce Harlow and Robert Merriam, in particular. Months passed, during which I wrote to or met with the responsible executives of seventeen voluntary agencies. Some were engaged in technical assistance, some in relief, and some in cultural exchange programs. All but four expressed interest in such a meeting.

One of the four insisted a "united front" already existed. But having attended its intermittent sessions, I knew that the bulk of its agenda consisted of such critical issues as how can we get the government to assume a larger share of the freight costs on the surplus grain and other materials we ship abroad? This clearly was not the sort of thing I had in mind.

Months passed. Finally, to my pleased surprise, I received notice that the president would see me precisely at noon on Thursday, May 12, 1960.

That day arrived—and with it the news that, eleven days earlier, Francis Gary Powers, piloting a U-2 "spy plane" for the CIA, had been shot down over the Soviet Union. Khrushchev was furious. Eisenhower was embarrassed. The longed-for summit conference was in jeopardy.

As I read the screaming headlines, I was certain my appointment would be canceled. Nevertheless, I spent most of the morning rehearsing what I hoped to say during the fifteen minutes that had been allotted to me.

It was raining. So at 11:30 I took a cab to the White House. There I was passed smoothly through the outer offices and down the checkerboard hallway to meet George V. Allen, former ambassador to India and Nepal, now the director of the United States Information Agency. We soon discovered we had a number of mutual friends, and I was pleased to learn that Mr. Allen would be my "host" and the only other attendant at the upcoming meeting.

As we entered the Oval Office, President Eisenhower rose slowly from behind his desk, more than a hint of tiredness reflected in his eyes. He had already met with his Cabinet that morning and had presented medals to some young achievers. But as George Allen introduced me the president managed his infectious smile and shook my hand so warmly I felt as if my appearance had really made his day.

"Sit down," he said, sinking back into his chair. "I'm afraid I don't know as much as I should about your program. Tell me about it."

Aware of the limits of my time, I described something of our purpose and operation as precisely as I could. The president seemed genuinely interested, breaking in at one point to tell me about a program he had recently visited in Latin America. It embodied the self-help principle. "The people were building their own homes, you see—using grooved wooden bricks, which they laid on concrete foundations that had already been poured by the government. The trouble was they nearly swamped me. *Everybody* wanted to have his brick autographed."

We laughed at the picture the story evoked.

"Go ahead," said the president, "tell me more."

I then described our basic philosophy and reported some of the results of our efforts.

Now the president sat up straight behind his desk, watching me intently.

"Mr. President," I said, leaning a bit closer, "I trust it will be no embarrassment to you if I state boldly what I know so many feel—that you hold a unique position in our world today."

His eyebrows raised, and he looked at me quizzically.

"You are, first of all, the man who led one of history's greatest invasions; you are the leader of a major political party; and for the last eight years you have been the head of our nation."

The president seemed a bit restive. Ambassador Allen beat a silent tattoo on the desk with the fingers of his left hand. Was I sounding like a hopeless sycophant? I hurried on.

"But you are also regarded as an idealist, a man who sincerely desires peace. Your prayers, your messages, your personal warmth have won you an exceptional place in the hearts of men. Certainly the mass reception you received in India, the Philippines, and South America is proof enough of this. You are now regarded as a man who is preeminently interested in people *as people*. Your advocacy of the ongoing program has made that clear."

At this point Ambassador Allen broke in to say that this had certainly been reflected at a recent meeting in London.

Apparently surprised to hear all this, the president expressed his regret that People to People had not reached the dimensions he had hoped for: "It just became a sort of free-for-all, with a lot of committees and activities that took the name *People to People*."

Then he stopped, waiting for me to continue.

I cleared my throat and plunged on. "In a few months, sir, you will be moving into private life. No one could blame you if you chose to put aside all further thoughts of public service. But I do feel impressed to say that, as you leave office, you carry on your shoulders the hopes of a great segment of the world's people. They have been inspired by your challenges to build a better world. They know, as you do, that these hopes are still to be realized."

The president listened pa .ently. The expression on Ambassador Allen's face was inscrut ble.

"Until now, Mr. P. esident, your career has been primarily military and political You have been engaged in 'holding the line,' as you once put : . in seeing that the 'negative' job was accomplished. Now, as you leave the presidency, you have the opportunity—and perhaps the duty—of leading the 'constructive' forces of the world. Where that 'constructive' program is most needed is in the under-developed areas."

I told him of the agencies that had indicated a willingness to meet together and to consider some sort of unified operation under his leadership, nominal or otherwise.

The president seemed favorably impressed. It was all I needed to ask the question that had brought me there.

"I would hope, Mr. President, that if such a 'unified front' *could* be brought into being, you would offer yourself—or at least be available—to give it the leadership and encouragement it would require."

The president looked straight ahead for a moment; then he rose from his chair and began to walk across the room. His hands thrust deep into his pockets, he gazed out on the White House lawn. He turned back to Ambassador Allen, then to me.

"You may not realize how many demands are being made on my time," he said. "Right now, some publishers are after me to write up the events of the last eight years. A great many other things are being laid before me."

He sat down and flexed his fingers.

"Since nineteen forty-one," he said slowly, "I have been in the position where I had either to take the initiative or accept the primary responsibility. Now, I'm not tired, but I just feel that I'm 'pumped out.' All Mamie and I would like to do for the first few months after I leave this office is to meet no schedule at all—just to let one day at a time determine what the day's program shall be. If I do get involved in any such activity as you describe—and it does appeal to me—I don't want to feel that I am the 'prime mover.'

"Incidentally," he said, "what would be the difference between the group you are now proposing and the group I called together in November of 1956?"

"The essential difference as I see it," I replied, "would be that this time, instead of seeking to arouse and enlist, instead of trying to persuade reluctant people to get involved, you would be *mobilizing* already-proven dedication and competence. The people I am asking you to think about are heads of agencies that are, for the most part, nonsectarian and nongovernmental in character and international in scope—agencies that are actually *doing* something, not just talking about it."

The president turned to Ambassador Allen.

"Why don't we act on this? We could call these groups in and set aside a couple of rooms here for two, maybe three, days. We could have the meeting in mid-December, after the elections. What do you think about it?"

The ambassador was on the spot. As director of the USIA, he was the de facto head of People to People. He must not have been happy with some of the things he had heard. *Should he now encourage something that might appear competitive?* I wondered.

He did not, however, raise any objections. So the president continued. "Follow through on this," he said to Mr. Allen. "Peters will give you the list of names and agencies. Your office can contact them. You can let me know how things go."

Then President Eisenhower turned back to me.

"Now I wouldn't want to take the leadership on whatever might develop," he said, "but the invitation can go out over my signature. I can be present and give it a boost every now and then, if I am asked. I can show up for various meetings, if I'm called upon. In general I can give it my encouragement and help."

He moved forward in his chair. "I hope you'll keep this on a practical, working basis—a limited staff, no highly paid executives. If you do, I'm acquainted with a number of people who have more money than they know what to do with. They'd surely be interested in helping."

I was watching for signs that we should be leaving. The conference had been scheduled for fifteen minutes. It had already run for twenty-six. But the president seemed in no hurry to be rid of us.

It was Ambassador Allen who finally stood to mark the end of the interview. The president rose with us; we walked to the door.

"Mr. President," I said, "I apologize if I have been trying to persuade you to do something that will add any further burden to those you already carry."

His reply was swift. "On the contrary, I don't want you to feel, by anything I've said, that I'm trying to get out of my part in anything I should do. If you get something going, such as this 'united front' you've talked about, and they want me to accept a role in some honorary capacity. . . . Well, let's say I would consider it."

This was, I felt, as far as any man—especially the president of the United States—could be expected to go. No man volunteers to give leadership to a program whose existence and constituency are yet to be determined.

I thanked the president. We shook hands and parted.

As we stepped outside the door, Ambassador Allen turned to me. "Well," he said, "the president has given you carte blanche."

He asked to be excused while he turned back for a few last words.

Minutes later I was walking down Nineteenth Street. The rain had ceased. But my head was in the clouds. Why not? By what I took to be an executive order, my hopes had been confirmed and my labors rewarded. "There is . . . a time to mourn," said Solomon in the Book of Ecclesiastes, "and a time to dance." *This* was the time to dance.

I followed through as the president suggested. But days passed, and weeks dragged by. June, as it usually does, followed May. And

July followed June. I departed on a tour of projects in Asia, asking my staff to keep a sensitive ear to possible developments. We heard very little.

Word finally came that the USIA wanted to include all the People to People projects and their affiliates in the proposed December meeting. I vigorously protested.

More time elapsed. Less news emerged. Would there actually be a meeting? When I discovered the matter had been tabled I could hardly get over my disbelief and outrage. But some group of functionaries had feared such a meeting might embarrass the incoming administration and had made the decision on that basis. It became apparent that ours is, at bottom, a government of bureaucracies.

When the elections were over, the president sent word asking when I could be back to see him. And a letter from Senator H. Alexander Smith, plus a note from Bob Merriam, told me that he was hopeful I would continue the effort to create a "united front."

But the "open sesame" for such a gathering would have been an invitation from the White House. With the Eisenhowers no longer at 1600 Pennsylvania Avenue, that persuasive charm was gone.

So ended my assault on Mount Olympus. It was "back to the boondocks." Our ongoing problems, not the incoming administration, was my assignment. I prepared once more to hit the trail.

Before I could get away, I received a letter from Congressman Henry Reuss—one of whose committee assignments was foreign operations. "As you know, " he wrote, "there is a growing interest across the country in the idea of a Youth Corps, whereby young Americans, college trained, fight hunger, disease and poverty in the underdeveloped areas of the world. Early this year the Congress approved a bill sponsored by the late Senator Neuberger and myself which authorized a study of this idea. Senator Hubert Humphrey later introduced a bill making detailed proposals, and during the campaign President-elect Kennedy made the Youth Corps an integral part of his proposed program.

"Because of your interest and experience in foreign assistance projects, I am writing to invite you to attend a discussion meeting here in Washington on Tuesday, December 20th." I was happy to note that Senator Humphrey cited a project near Assiut, Egypt, as an example of what he had in mind. Begun in 1953, that project had been a joint effort of World Neighbors and International Voluntary Services. Egypt's government had highly acclaimed our modest, nongovernmental, and genuinely grass-roots effort.

We were grateful that, for Senator Humphrey at least, what we had done at Assiut was what he wanted to have the government do worldwide. But it dawned on me that all this preliminary work on the youth corps was undoubtedly the reason why my proposal for a "united front" of voluntary agencies had never really had a chance. I had a hard time not feeling resentful, because what I had proposed would complement, not compete with, any governmental youth corps. The two developments could have been mutually beneficial.

That was water over the dam; and Congressman Reuss had invited me to be at the planning conference for the new project. I felt I had to accept.

Prior to the meeting, and in keeping with the congressman's request, I had prepared a five-page memorandum of suggested principles, policy, program, and personnel. Replies from Hubert Humphrey, Bill Moyers (who would become deputy director of the Peace Corps), and others assured me that the recommendations were on target.

Still, as we gathered in the large Banking and Currency Committee Room (part of the congressman's bailiwick), I wondered, as I listened to the cacophony, *Was this trip* really *necessary?*"

One of the first men to speak, tired of the punctilious preliminaries, got the floor by simply rising to his feet and waiting to be recognized.

"Mr. Chairman," he thundered, pounding the air to emphasize his earnestness, "unless we send over two hundred thousand of these young people, we are making a laughingstock of the whole idea. This has got to be impressive. And that means big!"

And that means trouble in more than River City, I thought. For he proposed an exportable Civilian Conservation Corps—an army of young people who would go into the underdeveloped areas to build roads, clear forests, improve port facilities, and do "public works." The ends were laudable but the means were dismal. For the last thing needed in the underdeveloped areas was a giant, alien, "work gang" coming over to preempt or displace the vast pool of underemployed nationals who needed any work that might become available.

A gray-haired objector gained the floor. Citing his experience in overseas operations, he pointed out the psychological and political dangers of moving en masse into foreign and sensitive areas.

The objection didn't faze the first man. Thrusting out his chin, he rasped, "I'm not exactly without experience myself. I belonged to an overseas youth corps for a while. They called us the Marines!"

Even so, he failed to carry his point. The final consensus was that the Youth Corps would be modeled on lines differing in considerable degree from the Marine Corps. After all, it was agreed—though one loud no kept it from being unanimous—the idea wasn't to *invade* an area, even to do it good.

With a general structure indicated, the assembling of the nuts and bolts was assigned to a battery of specialists, chosen largely from educational institutions whose facilities and curricula seemed appropriate.

Satisfied and gratified, I went home.

One of President John F. Kennedy's first official acts was the establishment of this new entity as perhaps the brightest star of his administration. In the years to come I would thank God for the Peace Corps. For it not only introduced thousands of Americans—mostly young ones—to the realities of the so-called Third World, it actually permitted some of them to make a significant difference.

Most of all, from an admittedly selfish perspective, it proved to be a real boon to World Neighbors. For it was the arena of basic training for an executive director, a vice-president for Overseas Program, and several area representatives.

If one of my dreams had to be scuttled for such accomplishments, I could well afford the sacrifice.

Epilogue

In 1961 a generous invitation from the P. X. Johnston family, who gave property and helped erect a headquarters building, brought us back to Oklahoma City. And it was none too soon. For trying to tell skeptical Burmese or Nigerians that the organization I represented—headquartered in Washington, D. C.—was strictly nongovernmental had become an exercise in futility. Oklahoma, on the other hand seemed unmistakably grass roots. The move eased tensions, saved money, and encouraged support. Across the succeeding years our overseas staff, relieved of a serious calumny, steadily expanded their outreach. So by some opportune interventions, a sizable amount of learning and labor, a handful of discriminating decisions, and a lot of "dumb luck"—the organism that was born in 1951 has made a meaningful contribution to the concept and process of what is called "development."

Yet we have entered only the vestibule of the house of need. For on our globe today, almost a billion men, women, and children exist under conditions of deprivation that are inconceivable to the average citizen of the affluent West. Yet as I learned so long ago, we, the propertied, and they, the beggared, are costewards of whatever future we pass on to our sons and daughters.

What, then, shall we do with this responsibility?

We can, as some do, merely sentimentalize it. We can write songs about it—and hope somehow it will go away. We can analyze its causes—and expect someone, not us, to deal with those causes. We can even travel to the Third World, to see its slums and smell its sweltering misery—and return to "recount our adventures." Or like my seatmate on the plane from Djakarta, we can hope "another war will straighten things out."

Finally, if we choose to recognize this imperative obligation, we can delegate it. Isn't fighting world hunger and poverty the task of some powerfully endowed body, like the Agency for International Development or the World Bank?

Well, they've tried, at staggering costs to the public treasury. What have been the results?

On February 21, 1989, Alan Woods, director of AID, reported: "The reality is that there have been no graduates from less-developed to developed in 20 years," and he concluded that United States aid promoted not development but dependence.[1] Perhaps we should have listened to Eric Sevareid when he said years ago, "Trying to pour money through the bureaucracies is like trying to pour money through blotting paper."

In 1974, as billions were being poured into projects in the Less Developed Countries, Robert McNamara, president of the World Bank, told his board of directors as they met in Nairobi: "The sad truth is that in most countries, the centralized administration of scarce resources—both money and skills—has usually resulted in most of them being allocated to a small group of the rich and powerful."[2]

In April, 1989, Walter Wriston, retired chairman of Citicorp, said: "The World Bank lent $150 million to Argentina in December or January. That was all on deposit in a Miami bank in 10 days."[3]

In sum, if we are to reach and energize the grass roots, we are going to have to find alternatives to governmental channels. Governments administer; *people* minister. Banks transfer funds and change currencies; *people* transform spirits and change attitudes. Therefore only "we the people" can successfully accomplish this huge, daunting task.

Our primary need is not more billions or bigger bulldozers. It is rather the mobilization and transmission of attitudes and technologies that—in the skillful hands of those who are enabled by competence, leavened by humility, and energized by love—can work miracles. For field-tested capability, coupled with the kind of hard-nosed love that evokes responsible affection, can create among potential partners a synergism that will bring about results which neither—nor both—of them can bring about independently.

That was my instinctive feeling forty years ago. It is my settled conviction today. Changes in the lives of millions of people attest its validity.

Behold, this was the iniquity of thy sister Sodom, pride, fulness of bread, and abundance of idleness was in her and in her daughters, neither did she strengthen the hand of the poor and needy.

Ezekiel 16:49

And the King shall answer and say unto them, Verily I say unto you, Inasmuch as ye have done it unto one of the least of these my brethren, ye have done it unto me.

Matthew 25:40

Notes

Prologue

1. John L. Peters, *Cry Dignity!* (Oklahoma City, Okla.: World Neighbors, 1976).

Chapter 2: The Testing Ground

1. "No Grain Shortage in Rajasthan—Minister's Reply to Debate in Lok Sabha," *The Sunday Statesman* (December 2, 1963).
2. S. Radhakrishnan, *East and West* (London: George Allen & Unwin, 1955), 129–130.
3. The Ahmadnagar College story was previously given in my book *Cry Dignity!* (Oklahoma City: World Neighbors, 1976), 21–24.
4. "Breakthrough in Birth Control," *New York Times* (October 20, 1974). Italics added.
5. "International Economic Survey," *New York Times* (February 8, 1981).
6. In the mid-1980s a psyllid (a jumping louse called heteropsylla cubana) began to attack the leucaena trees—first in Florida, then the Hawaiian Islands, then in Indonesia, the Philippines, and South India. By 1986–1987 the effect had become completely devastating.

     Three avenues of counterattack were considered: insecticides, predatory insects, and plant diversification (such as Calliandra and Gliricidia). The first two approaches involved large costs and serious risks. The third is now being applied on a worldwide scale. World Neighbors is heavily involved in this diversification in Nepal, India, and Indonesia. Prospects are promising.

Chapter 3: We Reach Out to Africa

1. A. J. Barker, *The Civilizing Mission* (New York: Dial Press, 1968), 325.
2. *Ethiopia Herald* (November 12, 1960).
3. *Insight* (May 4, 1987), 37.
4. A report from Canterbury was to say, "The Uganda Province of the church has increased its baptized membership from 1.3 million to 2.1 million . . . since the last Lambeth Conference. . . . By comparison, the Episcopal Church in the United States has lost half a million" (*New York Times* [July 30, 1975]).
5. Paul Johnson, *Modern Times* (New York: Harper & Row, 1983), 536.

Chapter 4: Return to Southeast Asia

1. The response I once received in New Delhi is a case in point.

In the mid-1950s, Public Law 480 (sometimes called "Food for Peace") stated that surplus grain from the United States could be "sold" to needy countries not already trading in those commodities with the United States, for local currencies. The accumulated funds could then be used by the United States for nonmilitary programs and projects within the host country. It was a stratagem designed to relieve the American market and to palliate recipient sensibilities.

In time, the United States "rupee account" reached such a level that, if actually spent, it would have thoroughly disrupted the Indian economy. Meanwhile, Senator Hubert Humphrey pushed through an amendment stating that 5 percent of these accounts could be used by private agencies engaged in relief or rehabilitation programs.

Since we were involved in numerous grass-roots development projects in India and all funds would go directly to local personnel, I felt we could use some of the United States rupees without jeopardizing our independence of action. A visit to the American embassy disabused me of that notion.

"Would it be possible," I asked, "for us to get some of those surplus rupees to pay our Indian associates?"

"Not a chance," said the clean-cut young attaché.

"Why?"

"Well, the agreement was that we would fund no projects which had not been approved by the minister under whose department it would fall. And these ministers will not approve anything they do not initiate."

I took a moment to let that sink in.

"Now let me get this straight. Whose money *is* this, anyway?"

"Technically," he said, "this fund is ours. But we have to lean over backward out here not to offend."

2. In the winter of 1988–1989, Felix and several others were seized by a band of Moro guerrillas and held for fifty-four days. During his imprisonment, Felix taught his illiterate captors to read.

3. The crash scene has been variously identified. In his book *The Magsaysay Story*, Carlos Romulo reported it as Cabalasan Peak (*see* p. 311). In Cebu, I was told it was actually Mount Manungal.

4. *Foreign Affairs* (April, 1966), 501.

5. Successful land reform requires: real ownership, in major degree paid for over a period of time by the cultivator; reasonable access to credit and markets; and effective assistance by qualified "county agents."

Chapter 5: Splendid Challenge—Splintered Response

1. Quoted in address by Alan A. Reich, deputy assistant secretary for educational and cultural affairs, *Department of State Bulletin* (May 31, 1971), 706.

Chapter 6: Opportunities South of Our Border

1. *Newsweek* (August 7, 1978), 73A.

2. "Rescue Consultant," *Wall Street Journal* (December 17, 1968), 14.

3. *Local Organizations and Rural Development, Volume Two: Case Studies*, A Report by Development Alternatives, Incorporated, to Development Support Bureau, Agency for International Development (Washington, D. C.: ATSOI, 1979), 166–169 passim.

4. Ibid., 170.

5. "The Atlantic Report," *Atlantic Monthly* (April, 1963), 19.

6. "Report of the Inter-American Commission on Human Rights on the Situation of Human Rights in the Republic of Guatemala,"

Organization of American States, General Assembly (October 14, 1981), 35, 36, 132.

7. *Central America Report* (February 4, 1983), 34.
8. *El Grafico* (May 20, 1982), 1.
9. *World Vision* (October 1982), 277.
10. *Wall Street Journal* (March 15, 1985), 25.
11. Roland Bunch has gathered these principles and practices into a book that is recognized as perhaps the definitive text on how you do agricultural development. Published in English, Spanish, French, and Arabic, it is titled *Two Ears of Corn* and is now in use by forty-five universities and colleges around the world. (For copies—$7.95, plus $2.00 for shipping and handling—or any further information, write: World Neighbors, 5116 N. Portland, Oklahoma City, OK 73112.)

Epilogue

1. "US World Chief Calls for Reforms," *Christian Science Monitor* (February 2, 1989), 1.
2. Robert S. McNamara, *Address to the Board of Governors* (Washington, D.C.: International Bank for Reconstruction and Development, 1973), 18.
3. "Flight of Capital Lies at Root of Latin America Debt Crisis," *Christian Science Monitor* (April 7, 1989), 8.